Eggs and ashes

Eggs and ashes

Practical & liturgical resources
for Lent and Holy Week

Ruth Burgess & Chris Polhill

WILD GOOSE PUBLICATIONS

Contents of book © the individual contributors
Compilation © 2004 Ruth Burgess & Chris Polhill

First published 2004 by

Wild Goose Publications, 4th Floor, Savoy House, 140 Sauchiehall St, Glasgow G2 3DH, UK.
Wild Goose Publications is the publishing division of the Iona Community.
Scottish Charity No. SCO03794. Limited Company Reg. No. SCO96243.
www.ionabooks.com

ISBN 978-1-901557-87-9

Reprinted 2005, 2007, 2010

The publishers gratefully acknowledge the support of the Drummond Trust,
3 Pitt Terrace, Stirling FK8 2EY in producing this book.

A catalogue record for this book is available from the British Library.

Overseas distribution:
Australia: Willow Connection Pty Ltd, Unit 4A, 3-9 Kenneth Road, Manly Vale, NSW 2093
New Zealand: Pleroma, Higginson Street, Otane 4170, Central Hawkes Bay
Canada: Novalis/Bayard Publishing & Distribution, 10 Lower Spadina Avenue, Suite 400,
Toronto, Ontario M5V 2Z3

Printed by Bell & Bain, Thornliebank, Glasgow, UK

General contents

Contents in detail

Key to symbols	
✝	Prayer
Ꮲ	Reading
⁘	Biblical reflection
✍	Liturgy
((◎))	Responses
♫	Song
☒	Story
📖	Sermon

Key to symbols	
✞	Prayer
↝	Reading
⁙	Biblical reflection
▨	Liturgy
((○))	Responses
♪	Song
▧	Story
📖	Sermon

Maundy Thursday

Key to symbols	
✞	Prayer
✺	Reading
✢	Biblical reflection
✍	Liturgy
((○))	Responses
♫	Song
🖎	Story
📖	Sermon

Good Friday

Key to symbols

✝	Prayer
↷	Reading
⁝	Biblical reflection
✍	Liturgy
(((○)))	Responses
♫	Song
🐁	Story
📖	Sermon

Introduction

This book began as two pieces of work – a Lent discipline, written for The Year of Justice and Care in the Lichfield diocese, and a Stations of the Cross, written for a congregation in South Tyneside. From there it grew and grew.

Our intention has been for this to be a resource book, so while there are some complete liturgies included, most of the material consists of the stuff that liturgies are made of – stories, prayers, biblical reflections, songs and responses.

The material is arranged chronologically, and we have tried to classify it into types for ease of reference. There are also pieces that can be used in a number of contexts, according to local needs.

Our grateful thanks to all our contributors for the rich and imaginative material they have sent us. It has been a joy to edit this book.

Special thanks are due to a number of people; to Bernadette and Pete Atkins for proof reading and wise comments; to John Polhill for his encouragement; to Gary Polhill and Louise Hayward for their commitment to environmental issues; to Jane Darroch-Riley, Alex Thompson, Tri Boi Ta and Sandra Kramer at Wild Goose Publications for their support, skills and encouragement, and particularly to Neil Paynter for his sensitive and competent editing and cheery e-mails.

Working together has been a learning process for both of us. Working on a common task builds not only community, but also negotiating skills and books.

Ruth Burgess and Chris Polhill,
August 2004

For Bishop Mike and Bishop Peter
with thanks and love

Shrove Tuesday

A short liturgy for Shrove Tuesday

For this liturgy you will need the following ingredients: flour, salt, milk, an egg; and the following tools: a mixing bowl and a whisk.

Reader 1: Come with me, come wander, come welcome the world,
Where strangers might smile or where stones may be hurled;
Come leave what you cling to, lay down what you clutch
And find, with hands empty, that hearts can hold much.

Sing hey for the carpenter leaving his tools!
Sing hey for the Pharisees leaving their rules!
Sing hey for the fishermen leaving their nets!
Sing hey for the people who leave their regrets!

(by John Bell and Graham Maule)

Song: *Sing hey for the Carpenter (Heaven Shall Not Wait, Wild Goose Songs, Volume 1)*

Reader 2: We come to God as we are:
we come with a history of rights and wrongs,
we come with a past of shaky discipleship,
we come with the chequered mixture called life.

Reader 1: We long to stay with what is familiar,
to cling to the comfortable, the predictable;
to hold to the past, however painful;
to find our security in a world of our making.

Reader 2: But God calls us to move on:
to enter the place of reflection and change,
to be confronted and challenged with reality,
to encounter the life-giving presence within.

Readers 1 & 2 present the ingredients as they say:

Reader 1: So, we sift in some flour, regrets from the past,
laying to rest what we no longer need.

Reader 2: And we add a touch of salt, vital for flavour:
provocative sharpness of God's truth.

Reader 1:   We take an egg, symbol of new life,
        anticipating God-inspired possibilities.

Reader 2:   And we take some milk, like our ancestors of old:
        nourishment for the journey ahead.

A third person (Reader 3) adds the ingredients to the mixing bowl and does the mixing.

Reader 3:   We mix it all together
        to use up ingredients of the past,
        ready to move forward
        through tomorrow's Lenten beginnings.

        And as we share in this food,
        may we marvel at the glorious creation
        which, by God's grace,
        we are now and yet will become.
        AMEN

Judith Jessop, Broomhill Methodist Church Liturgy Group

This is an egg

(This is a performance poem and could be read by adults and/or children. The words in brackets could be written on signs to be held up by someone other than the readers, to encourage audience participation. Each verse of the poem could be read by a different reader, with all of the readers reciting the last verse together.)

This is an egg.
I can eat it.
I can eat it raw (YUK!)
I can eat it scrambled
coddled
fried
soft-boiled
hard-boiled or
poached.

This is an egg.
I can use it to make cakes (YUM, YUM)

I can use it to make puddings
pastry
custard
biscuits
and pancakes.

This is an egg.
I can drop it (WHOOPS)
Its shell will break.
Inside it is all gooey and sticky.

This is an egg.
It's really easy to drop.
I can drop it in the kitchen
in the living room
down the stairs
behind the tele
on the floor.
Maybe the dog will lick it up. (WOOF WOOF)

This is an egg.
Birds lay eggs.
And so do snakes,
echidnas
and possibly dragons (WOW!)
and definitely duck-billed platypuses.

These are three eggs.
I could try to juggle with them … (BE CAREFUL)
But maybe I'll practise
with something else first.

Today is Shrove Tuesday (HOORAY)
Tomorrow is Ash Wednesday,
which is the beginning of Lent.
Long ago some Christians did not eat eggs during Lent.
Lent lasts for 40 days –
I wonder what the chickens did!*

Before Lent began
on Shrove Tuesday – which is today (HOORAY) –
the Christians cooked all their eggs and ate them.
They must have had
scrambled eggs
soft-boiled eggs
fried eggs
poached eggs
coddled eggs
and hard-boiled eggs.
And one year,
when there were still eggs left over,
someone tried mixing them with flour and milk
and invented …
pancakes (YUM, YUM)

And so, ever since on Shrove Tuesday,
which is today (HOORAY)
we make pancakes.
And we eat them with
sugar
lemon
syrup
jam
ice cream,
and onion gravy …
Just kidding.

We love pancakes
They are (YUM, YUM, YUM)
The end.

(* Long ago, chickens were older breeds and would not have laid eggs in the winter. On Shrove Tuesday, people would have been eating up the last of the preserved eggs, which were probably coming to the end of their preservation period. By Easter Day, the chickens would be starting to lay eggs again.)

Ruth Burgess

The desert waits
(an invitation to Lent)

The desert waits,
ready for those who come,
who come obedient to the Spirit's leading;
or who are driven,
because they will not come any other way.

The desert always waits,
ready to let us know who we are –
the place of self-discovery.

And whilst we fear, and rightly,
the loneliness and emptiness and harshness,
we forget the angels
whom we cannot see for our blindness,
but who come when God decides
that we need their help;
when we are ready
for what they can give us.

Ruth Burgess

Ash Wednesday

From dust we came

From dust we came,
to dust we will return
WE BELONG TO GOD

We gather in penitence,
we gather in confidence
WE BELONG TO GOD

At the beginning of Lent,
at every moment of our lives
WE BELONG TO GOD

Ruth Burgess

Marked by a cross

Marked by a cross,
cherished and forgiven
WE ARE TRAVELLING HOME

Called to be holy,
called to be happy
WE ARE TRAVELLING HOME

Across deserts,
over mountains
WE ARE TRAVELLING HOME

God in our hearts,
God in our lives
WE ARE TRAVELLING HOME

Ruth Burgess

Ash Wednesday responses from Iona

Choose this day

Choose this day whom you will serve;
WE WILL CHOOSE THE LIVING GOD.

The road is narrow that leads to life;
WE WILL WALK THE WAY OF CHRIST

Faith is not our holding on;
FAITH IS LETTING GO

We offer more than words, O God;
WE OFFER YOU OUR LIVES

We will follow you, O Christ
(Matthew 5:3–11)

(A and B could be two readers or two halves of the congregation.)

Leader: Jesus says to his disciples:
A: **Happy are you needy ones:**
B: **The kingdom of God is yours.**
A: **Happy are you who are hungry:**
B: **You will be satisfied.**
A: **Happy are you who weep now:**
B: **You will be filled with laughter.**
A: **Rejected, insulted, happy are you;**
B: **Be glad and dance with joy.**

Leader: Jesus said: Take up your cross.
ALL: WE WILL FOLLOW YOU, O CHRIST,
             INTO THE NEEDS OF THE WORLD,
             INTO THE TRUTH OF OUR LIVES,
             INTO THE PAIN OF OUR HEARTS,
             INTO THE PRESENCE OF GOD.
             AMEN

Brian Woodcock

Three prayers for Ash Wednesday

To you we shall return

Mysterious God, morning, noon and night
reveal your creative power;
around us the whole earth cries glory.
Your presence beats in our blood, children of creation!
Yet we go on our way deaf to the larks above the track,
looking down into the mud and not up into the clear sky.
And, even then, we miss the myriad small signs of hope:
the crocus opening its heart to the sun,
colours of sea-washed stones, rainbows in the mist.
We despair so easily. We say: 'Where is God in all this?'
And we deny it has any meaning. We say: 'God is dead.'
We cannot find or feel the pulse of your life in us.
We put our shaky faith in things we have made,
we give cringing power to the institutions.
We give up on ourselves, saying: 'We are no good.'
We live in a way that says: 'There is no God.'
And the song of creation turns to dust and ashes on our lips.
Forgive us.
Dust we are – and to dust we shall return.

But, in Jesus, you chose to share our human frailty,
to enter into our mortality in all its mystery,
to redeem this handful of dust.
We are yours – and to you we shall return. AMEN

How can I find my way back?

O God, where did I go wrong?
How can I find my way back?
I am weighed down by this feeling
that I have failed – you, other people, myself.
My life is a mess.

Kyrie eleison (sung or said)

You know my weakness.
You know much better than me:

I can't hide it from you.
How can I bear to face it too?

Kyrie eleison (sung or said)

Guilty as charged –
however much I argue my case.
It's your laws I have broken;
it's your way I have lost;
it's your word I have chosen not to hear
over and over again.

Kyrie eleison (sung or said)

O God, where did I go wrong?
How can I find my way back?

A time of turning round

Truly dust we are, and to dust we shall return;
and truly yours we are, and to you we shall return.
Help this to be a time of turning round and beginning again.
Through the forty days of Lent, help us to follow you
and to find you: in the discipline of praying
and in the drudgery of caring –
in whatever we deny ourselves,
and whatever we set ourselves to learn or do.
Help us to discover you
in our loneliness and in community,
in our emptiness and our fulfilment,
in our sadness and our laughter.
Help us to find you when we ourselves are lost.
Help us to follow you on the journey to Jerusalem
to the waving palms of the people's hope,
to their rejection, to the cross and empty tomb.
Help us to perceive new growth amid the ashes of the old.
Help us, carrying your cross, to be signs of your Kingdom. AMEN

Jan Sutch Pickard

Come back to God

A four-part chant for Ash Wednesday

(Words from Joel 2:12)

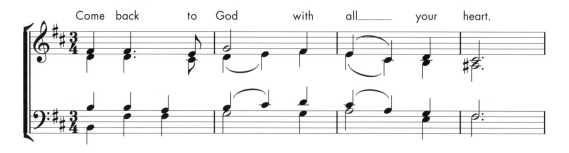

Emily J Walker

Ashes and penance

Ashes

– powdery-grey
from keeping on trying
to get a spark from two stones

– streaky black
from relighting a candle
that keeps going out

– soft white
from a fire that burned down to its heart
and kept everyone warm

these are ashes worth wearing

Penance

for self-absorption
– many hours in the company of three-year-olds

for carelessness
– a year's close study of an elder tree

for injustice
– giving thanks for the rain and sun
that fall on you anyway

for pride
– learning to see the funny side
of your coals of fire.

Kathy Galloway

Be our way, our truth, our life

Lord Jesus,
desert dweller,
help us now,
at this time of Lent,
to accompany you.

If we have grown soft,
cushioning our lives
with excuses,
expose us to the toughness
of your way.

If we have grown lazy,
cushioning our minds
with easy, thin thoughts,
expose us to the rigour
of your truth.

If we have grown comfortable,
cushioning our living
with satisfaction and success,
expose us to the challenge
of your life.

As we walk,
God, be our way.
As we learn,
God, be our truth.
As we grow
God, be our life.

We pray in Jesus' name. AMEN

John Harvey and Millicent

Lent discipline:
an environmental challenge

Making your lifestyle count
A Lent programme for Christians who care about the environment

Introduction

When Saint Columba sent his monks out from Iona to convert the peoples of northern Europe, his instructions to them were very simple: Go and settle in a community and let them see *the way that you live*. No door-to-door evangelism, no preaching on street corners; Columba felt that their lifestyle would speak for itself – and it did.

At the first World Summit on the Environment in Rio de Janeiro in 1992, the world powers, organisations and experts agreed that the best way forward on environmental issues is through local initiatives. At the summit they drafted Agenda 21, known for its motto: 'Think globally and act locally.'

Lent is traditionally a time for greater discipline in our lifestyles, in order to focus more on God's priorities. In 2003, the Bishop of Wolverhampton, Michael Bourke, spoke about wanting to explore environmental issues during Lent, because we now know that we have been living in a way that has damaged God's creation and need to change (repent). In response to Bishop Mike's concerns we developed this Lent discipline, which, of course, can be used as an environmental challenge at any time of the year.

Following the Lent discipline

In each of the six weeks of this Lent discipline there are suggested environmental actions for you to take on. Some are quite small things, some are challenging. Some are actions that you could do as a family or household, some are individual. You may well be doing some already.

Each week has a theme corresponding to one aspect of concern for the environment (transport, water, energy, waste, shopping thoughtfully, and improving biodiversity). You are invited to take on two or three items from the action list each week. If you feel able, you may want to try carrying on one of these items through the whole of Lent. But remember, *everything* that we do for the environment, however small, is a vital contribution and a witness to our belief in God the Creator; this environmental challenge is for you to experiment with, not to be oppressed by.

One of the most important contributions you can make to caring for the environment is to be informed about the issues. In the material for each week you will find a short list of actions for research and campaigning (for which you will need to be informed). There are some organisations listed on pages 71–72 that can help you with this.

The Internet is a powerful (if occasionally frustrating) source of information. If you don't have your own modem connection you can access the Internet at most public libraries for free. You could decide to spend, say, an hour each week doing research on the Internet as one of your three items.

You may find it helpful to keep a diary of the actions you decided to take, and the problems and benefits that you experienced.

Throughout the Lent discipline there are prayers and other worship resources to help you focus. Also included are some stories from the Intermediate Technology Development Group (ITDG). ITDG was conceived by E.F. Schumacher and helps people to use technology in the fight against poverty. ITDG works in partnership with communities to develop practical answers to their problems, based on local knowledge and skills and putting people's needs first.[1]

The ITDG stories in the Lent discipline are about alternative options to the high technology we take for granted.

A prayer to begin with:

From quark to planet

Creator God,
from quark to planet your universe is awesome.
Give us eyes to gape at the wonders daily about us,
and the will to live in the harmony of your creating.
Help us to recognise and honour the connections of all things,
even at cost to our own wants and comforts;
so we may live gently on earth,
and all creation praise you. Amen

Chris Polhill

Week one – use of transport

We all know that petrol and diesel engines burn irreplaceable fossil fuels and that short journeys have high fuel consumptions. High altitude flying dumps greenhouse gases directly into the upper atmosphere. We expect to buy all kinds of fruit and vegetables at any time of year. Our attitude to transport is costing the earth.

Actions

Choose two or three of these:

- Walk or cycle everywhere
- Cut your car journeys by X%
- No car journeys less than one mile
- Replace your car with a second-hand model, and one that has a lower CO_2 output
- Use public transportation whenever practicable
- Car share whenever possible – school run, work, shopping trips
- Sell your car and buy a bicycle
- Commit not to travel by air this year

Research and campaigning

Choose one of these:

- Look at the country of origin of the food you buy and choose items that have travelled less
- Campaign for wider use of bio-diesel (fuel made from vegetable oils)

At jet speed or walking pace

Holy God, you see all our needs
and know the desires of our hearts.
In our journeys,
whether at jet speed or walking pace,
may we know you beside us
and follow your direction.

Chris Polhill

The contradictions of our lives

Lord God, we pray about the contradictions in our lives:

Aircraft and automobiles produce pollution. You have made us trustees of planet Earth, and look to us to preserve clean air. Should we pray and act against these polluting agents?

But you have also set us in families, and given us friends across the world. Loving relationships are better nourished when people meet. So, we give thanks for the means of putting us in touch with each other, and pray that we may find ways to reduce pollution.

Ian M Fraser

The gift of travel

Freedom to see families,
hold them close, see their homes;
freedom to visit friends,
laughing, talking in their company;
freedom to stare at mountain peaks,
see the sea, the waterfall, the forest;
thank you, Lord.

Thank you
for bike and boat and plane,
for car and coach and train,
for maker, inventor, travel agent.
Thank you for the precious gift of travel.

Teach us to use it wisely.
God, teach us to use it wisely.

Chris Polhill

Cyclist's prayer

Thank you, gracious God,
for the privilege of pedalling,
for the chance to see so much more,
for the opportunity to stop and talk
or look and listen,
for the exultation of racing down hills,
for the increased fitness of struggling up them.
Keep me committed when it is wet or windy.
Thank you, gracious God, for bicycles. Amen

Andrew De Smet

Forgive us our failing

Leader: We yearn to heal the damage to the world our actions have caused, yet
we are afraid of the changes needed and wish to guard our lifestyles. We
are divided within our souls and need God's healing.

Let us confess our sins:

ALL: FOR UNRESTRAINED ECONOMIC GROWTH,
FOR CONSPICUOUS CONSUMPTION,
FOR ALWAYS WANTING MORE,
FORGIVE US OUR FAILING.

FOR MORE AND MORE CARS,
FOR BURNING ENERGY WITHOUT THOUGHT,

FOR WANTON WASTE,
FORGIVE US OUR FAILING.

FOR NOT THINKING THROUGH CONSEQUENCES,
FOR NOT CARING FOR FUTURE GENERATIONS,
FOR BLIND INDIFFERENCE,
FORGIVE US OUR FAILING.

Silence

Leader: The forgiveness of the Maker, who knows you, be yours;
the forgiveness of the Son, who knows life's struggles, be yours;
the forgiveness of the Spirit, who encourages, be yours;
the love of God, who enables life-giving change,
be yours today and always.

ALL: CREATOR GOD,
REDEEMER SON,
GUIDING SPIRIT,
HELP US TO LIVE RESPONSIBLY
IN YOUR WORLD. AMEN

Andrew De Smet and Chris Polhill

A travelling prayer

Praise you,
journeying God;
God of movement,
God of change.

Thank you for the example of Jesus,
who travelled lightly,
taking note of creation along the way.

Our expectations now are for holidays in outer space.
Travel – a right not to be interfered with.
Our eyes are blind to the impact of our travelling on others
and on the life of the planet.

Thank you for the beautiful places around us.
Help us to treat them gently,
appreciate them,
and learn to care for them.

And may we rediscover what Jesus practised:
to travel lightly
and to walk with friends.

Jo Rathbone

Transporting goods Sudanese-style
(Story from ITDG)

Intermediate means of transport are rural transport options that lie between buses and cars, and walking. They include animal-drawn carts, bicycles, cycle trailers and wheelbarrows. To facilitate their use paths and roads sometimes need widening. In rural Sudan people walk long distances on narrow paths. Here ITDG realised the importance of animal-drawn carts and trained metal workers to manufacture wheels and transport devices. Previously people had reused car wheel rims, but these did not last long. The ITDG cart design proved to be more durable, especially the wheels and hubs. The metal workers increased their income by making the carts; people who owned the carts rented them out to carry people, goods and water. The carts are a cheaper alternative for moving goods than taxis and pick-up cars; many more villages have been connected to markets and services.

Adapted from *Practical Answers to Poverty*

Week two – use of water

It's rare for us to experience water shortage, and when we do we tend to blame it on the water companies. Unlimited supply of drinking water is still an un-attainable luxury in many parts of the world. By avoiding excessive use of water we help to ensure that supplies in this country are sufficient without the creation of more reservoirs and we remind ourselves of the many people in our world who have no access to clean drinking water – let alone the chance to flush the toilet with it!

Actions

Choose two or three of these:

- Fix dripping taps
- Turn off the tap while brushing your teeth
- Have a shower rather than a bath
- Shower less than 2 minutes per day
- Turn the shower off while soaping
- Wash your car using a bucket (not a hose pipe)
- Only do full washing loads
- Use economy settings on washing machines
- Don't wash clothes unnecessarily
- Wash up in large batches
- Only run the dishwasher when it's full
- Replace your toilet's flushing mechanism with a modern low-water-consumption design
- Get a 'hippo' for the loo/Place a brick in the cistern
- Don't wash the car
- Collect rain water for use in your garden

Research and campaigning

Choose one of these:

- Research the amount of water used in making products so that you can avoid products manufactured with an intensive use of water
- Investigate installing a rain water system to flush the loo (and for washing clothes)

Living water

We are connected in creation
by water which gives us life.

Tides move in our blood,
and on distant shores
our kindred lift their heads
in the salt air
and scan the horizon
for a trace of our mark on the earth.

Let our marks be gentle.
Let us respect the sacredness of water
which moves between us
as a blessing from the hand of God.

Yvonne Morland

Water

Water trickling down the hillside,
hiding under grass and stones,
brown as earth and soft as kisses,
tumbling, sparkling, free it goes.

Water trickling down the faces,
precious drops evaporate
on the silent heads of children,
water falling far too late.

Down the rivers water flowing,
endless cycle from the sea,
siphoned into busy cities,
lifeblood of our industry.

Water flowing deep beneath us,
buried in the earth and clay,

but the crops are parched and shrivelling
and the well is dry today.

Water raging at the coastline,
sense the rhythm of the storm;
see the beauty, feel the power
watched from safety, light and warm.

Water raging down the river
spreading over fields in sheets,
tearing houses, drowning cattle,
sweeping through the city streets.

Jesus shared a stranger's water;
for our thirst the cross he bore,
bringing for us living water
so the world need thirst no more.

Can we share our precious water,
letting others' needs come first,
working, praying for a future
when the world need never thirst?

Alix Brown

Clean water

Bless the Almighty, O my soul.
O God, my Creator, how mighty art Thou!
Your power is like deep oceans.
Your blessings shower us daily like rain from the sky.
Your love is abundant like waves on the shore.
Thank you for water to cleanse and revive us.

Yet drought kills millions of your people;
will there come a time when there's not enough water for all?
I see swimming pools as luxury; clean, fresh water wasted
in a land where many quench their thirst with dirty water.

Inspire those who govern to prioritise clean water:
spending a little to save many lives.
Open the showers of heaven to soften barren land.
Shower us with your love that softens hardened hearts.

Richard Moeketsi Thito

A water blessing

May clean, clear water bless us,
wellspring or waterfall,
life in abundance
flowing, cleansing, refreshing.

May we use wisely
God's gift of water
and cherish each drop;
bring life to Earth's deserts

Jesus, pour your water,
greening and satisfying,
on the dry dustiness
of the deserts within us.

Holy Spirit, flow through us;
revive our faithfulness,
cleanse our sinfulness,
fill us with prayerfulness.

Chris Polhill

Water stories and prayers

In the mid-nineteenth century, the more affluent citizens of Glasgow became aware that the waterborne diseases that resulted when the poor took buckets of water from the polluted Clyde did not stop at their gates. By 1859 they had found the remedy – water piped from Loch Katrine. It reached the homes of rich and poor with transforming effect. Water pipes were like the hands of Christ, stretched over intervening miles to provide health.

Prayer

Give thanks for the rain, so often treated as the poor relation of the sun.
Give thanks for planners, construction firms, plumbers, who bring water long distances into homes.
Give thanks for the people who invigilate the quality of water.
Pray that all people may have clean water.

In Latin America, a guerrilla stands in a river, her rifle lying within reach on the bank. She has not removed any clothes, but is exhilarated by the rush of water penetrating them to wash out dirt and to refresh her tired body. O, the joy on her face – the long weeks of mud and watchfulness temporarily behind her!

Prayer

Give thanks for clouds, rivers, lochs, seas, the great gifts of creation, which we can use well or badly but cannot contrive.
Give thanks for baths, showers, bathing, which cleanses the body, draws out weariness from the bones, refreshes people for whatever awaits them.
Pray for people in shanty towns, in cramped accommodation, deprived of access to clean water.
Pray for fire fighters confronting house and forest fires.
Pray for protesters braving water cannons.

In Bungsipsee in Chaiyapoon province in Thailand, a Buddhist/Christian student work camp is building water tanks, one each in four neighbouring villages. At no great distance there is a stream which could be dammed to make a small reservoir adequate to meet all their needs. Village labour could construct it. Were the villagers lazy? the students from the city wondered.

Then they learned the truth of the matter: There was a strong-man in the neighbour-hood whose thugs would have waited until the work was finished, taken it over, and then sold to the villagers the water that the villagers had worked to make available.

Prayer

Pray for situations where the powerful exploit water resources to the disadvantage of the weak.

Ian M Fraser

Crescent-shaped terraces
(Story from ITDG)

ITDG worked closely with farmers in North Darfur (Sudan) to assist them in over-coming food shortages. One approach was to increase water infiltration. Tradition-ally, terraces for water harvesting were mostly rectangular in shape and not high enough for current needs. ITDG offered training in simple survey techniques so that farmers could detect the direction of the slope and ways of protecting the terrace from being washed away if not well drained. Crescent-shaped terraces with slightly higher edges were tried. These captured and spread more water, and resis-ted water erosion by allowing excess water to flow through the edges of the cres-cent. Now farmers harvest vegetables for six months after the rainy season and earn money and secure food, even during seasons of low rainfall.

Adapted from ITDG *Practical Answers to Poverty*

Stemming the flood waters in Bangladesh
(Story from ITDG)

In Bangladesh, floods devastate the country every year. In the poorest areas, houses are washed away and people face the daunting task of rebuilding them. ITDG has worked with the local community to develop an improved house design to ensure homes withstand the floods. The house consists of a room for sleeping and storage and a veranda for cooking, with windows opposite the veranda to improve ventilation. Within the room a raised bamboo platform provides storage for valuables in the severest floods. A plinth of soil, stones and cement raises the whole house above ordinary flood levels. The main structure of the house is made from concrete footings and bamboo posts treated against rot; these are held together with metal ties, bracings and fasteners. The walls of the house are made of jute matting, which is cheap and easy to replace.

Adapted from *Small World* magazine

Week three – use of energy

The electricity, gas and fuel oil we use in our homes come mostly from fossil fuels. For most of us there is no realistic alternative, but we can be responsible about our consumption of energy and adapt our lifestyles to reduce our use of fossil fuels. There are electricity suppliers who will guarantee to supply customers from renewable sources of energy (usually at no added cost). If you have investment capital, you can install solar PV (electric) panels, with a moderate rate of financial return under the current grant scheme.

Actions

Choose two or three of these:

- Keep your windows and doors closed
- Only fill up the kettle to the amount of water required
- Hang your clothes to dry instead of using the tumble dryer
- Turn your central heating down and wear warmer clothes
- Only heat the room you are using
- Use eco light bulbs
- Don't leave appliances on stand-by
- Turn off garden water features and outside lights or install PIR detectors
- Avoid cooking in a conventional oven (use a hob or investigate methods such as hay boxes)
- Improve your home's insulation
- Reduce the amount of hot water you use
- Switch your energy provider to one that uses renewable energy sources
- Give up using your TV and computers
- Go to bed at sunset and get up at dawn

Research and campaigning

Choose one of these:

- Consider installing a solar PV (electric) or a solar water system
- Research the use of energy in the manufacture of the goods you buy, and the amount of energy used in transporting them
- Look into replacing existing appliances with energy efficient (A rated) ones
- Write to your MP about streetlight pollution

Lord of energy, teach us to pray …

Our Creator,
source of all power,
we want to align ourselves like iron filings to your magnet.
We want to be drawn to your intent;
to live in a society that responds to your beckoning,
to feel the surge of your life-giving energy.
Grant us wisdom in our use of physical energy.
Help us to live by the standards we choose,
not those of others:
to focus our desire on you,
not the fake comforts of modern living;
to be satisfied by a sense of your love,
not our own power or status.
Because we know that your way is the only true way,
that everything we love and are is a gift from you,
and that to know you as our Creator
is to glimpse eternity.

John Polhill

The be-attitudes

Blessed are those who use low-energy light bulbs,
for theirs is the light of God's wisdom.

Blessed are those who travel by train,
for their lives are on God's track.

Blessed are those who choose a car with low fuel consumption,
for they are in God's fast lane.

Blessed are those who insulate their homes,
for theirs is the warmth of God's love.

Blessed are you when you put yourselves out
to use energy from renewable sources,
for you have kindled the flame of the future.

John Polhill

Our thoughtless wasting

For heat blasting in open doorways,
for lights burning in empty rooms,
for homes basking in T-shirt warmth,
forgive our thoughtless wasting.

For leaving windows draughty,
for lagging left undone,
for lofts uninsulated,
forgive our thoughtless wasting.

For cars that guzzle petrol,
for driving little journeys,
for cheaper fares on planes,
forgive our thoughtless wasting.

God grant us clear thinking, right action, and a gentle lifestyle. Amen

Chris Polhill

Choices

Oil spoils.
Coke chokes.
Gas – alas,
all will end.

Use

the sun or we're done;
the wind or we've sinned;
the wave that can save;
the tree growing free.

All ever present.
God-made,
God-given.

Chris Polhill

The parable of the churchgoer and the asylum-seeker

Jesus told this parable to people who were sure of their own lifestyle and despised everyone else:

'Once there were two men who went to the corner shop to buy a newspaper – one was a churchgoer, the other an asylum-seeker. The churchgoer stood apart by himself and thought: *I thank you, God, that I am not idle, sponging off the benefit system and the health service. I thank you that I am not like that asylum-seeker over there. I have provided for myself financially, I buy organic vegetables, I live in an energy-efficient house, and I tithe my income.*

The asylum-seeker stood at a distance with his head down and thought: *God, have mercy on me.*

'I tell you,' said Jesus, 'the asylum-seeker, and not the churchgoer, was in the right with God when he went home.'

John Polhill

To be ... satisfied

I've got no energy
because I've got too much energy,
rushing to and fro for things I don't need.

There's no cure but nothing.

I'll do nothing to save energy:
Sit, like a lily of the field,
and sway in the breeze.

Nothing to save myself:
I'll lose myself,
like a bird turning in turbulence.

All my life's work:
to achieve nothing and be satisfied.

Gary Polhill

Praise God

Praise God for the wind
whirling through the clouds,
fog and mist dispersing;
power turbine spinning;
energy creating.
Alleluia.

Praise God for sunlight
brightening the sky,
cold and dark destroying;
solar panels waking;
energy creating.
Alleluia.

Praise God for the sea tides
pulled by the moon,
wave and power displaying;
blade and cog revolving;
energy creating.
Alleluia.

Praise God for the tree
freshening the air,
green and ever-growing,
coppice woodland making;
energy creating.
Alleluia.

Praise God for people
watching for your way,
listening and working;
gentle footprints leaving;
energy revealing.
Alleluia.

Chris Polhill

The essence of banality

The miracle of photosynthesis,
a billion microscopic organisms
living and dying in the sea,
layer upon layer of sediment,
the pressure of aeons ......

A drill,
a pipe,
a trip to the shops,
a plastic bag.

Gary Polhill

Grid-free power
(Wind generation for developing countries)

Wind power is now providing energy for rural communities in developing countries. For people in rural areas, a few tens of watts of energy are sufficient for providing lighting and a source of power for a radio or television. Small wind machines in the 5-100 kilowatt range can supply this and form a small local power station. Batteries can be charged and used at home then returned to the power station for recharging. Battery recharging reduces the inconvenience of an intermittent energy supply due to fluctuating wind speeds. Small wind generators in the 50-500 watt range can also be used for individual household connection. During times when wind is insufficient, the system can be backed up by the use of diesel.

Adapted from *Hands On Winds of Change*

Week four – reducing waste and pollution

Landfill mountains have risen like monuments to our waste-making society. Councils who have introduced recycling schemes are to be praised, but, sadly, our national annual volume of waste is increasing faster than the amount going into recycling. Change is up to us. We have choices. We are responsible for the amount of waste we create and the way we dispose of it.

Actions

Choose two or three of these:

- Don't buy anything that has more than one wrapping
- Buy recycled products
- Avoid individually wrapped and bleached sanitary items
- Don't flush non-degradable items down the loo
- Use recycled bin liners, or don't use bin liners and wash out the rubbish container
- Set yourself a target for waste reduction
- Use only biodegradable detergents
- Measure and record the amount of rubbish that you don't reuse or recycle
- Don't buy anything that you can't eat or recycle in its entirety (including packaging).
- Compost your kitchen and garden waste
- Buy in bulk, if this reduces packaging and you can carry the items home
- Use organic products in your garden (fertilisers, weed control, pest control)
- Buy organic – avoid products from intensive farming.
- Repair products whenever possible

Research and campaigning

Choose one of these:

- Write to your MP about reducing our dependence on nuclear power
- Ask your local council about how it recycles – what it collects and why it doesn't collect more

Prayer of Franciscan conservation

Living God,
where there is waste, let us bring recycling;
where there is recycling, let us bring reuse;
where there is reuse, let us bring sustainability;
where there is sustainability, let us bring justice;
where there is justice, let us bring love.

John Polhill

Prayer at a supermarket checkout

God, my friend and creator, the person in front of me has bought a bag of bags of crisps and put them into a plastic carrier bag; does it matter?

Was this part of the Great Plan? Did the generous outpouring of your love in the moment that the universe began include the bag of bags of bags?

Did your wrath get used up in the Old Testament?

When the contents of that perfect, shiny bag have been eaten up, and that bag is deep in landfill, is it any better or worse than the fossil fuel from which it came?

And, if it is 50 million years since the death of the plant that became the fossil fuel, will another 50 million years make good of the crisp bags?

You're not going to tell me are you?

Because the plant, the oil, the bag, the 50 million years, and the moment at the checkout are all your gifts to me.

I pray for the grace to know that, and to wonder at it.

John Polhill

Objects

Everything has a past.
A journey through salt and grit.
Smoothed and roughened by winds and tides,
history in the stones and tangle.
A smell of pleasant death in the wood,
an inkling of memory in the polished pieces,
all of something bigger.
Chips, sparks and fragments from the monoliths of time.
We cannot ask their histories,
only guess
at the glimpse of sun-shafts, hooves and hammers
which have given shapes.
A future too,
sometimes edible,
sometimes ornamental,
nothing is disposable here.

Judith Jardine

Waster wannabe

Get me
    I don't give an alu can
        For your eco-speako
Get me
    I eat half my chips
        Chucked the rest on the verge
            Helps to make jobs for litter-pickers
                Puts a bit of blossom in yer hedge bottom
Get me
    I turn on all the lights
        Bang up the music
            Shove my foot on the gas
                Live in the fast lane
                    Couldn't give an eco-hoot

Get me
　　You never will
　　　　Or make me want to care
　　　　　Or share
　　　　　　Your eco-attitudes
　　　　　　　Until I feel
　　　　　　　　You care for me.

John Polhill

Reusing

Jesus our Saviour,
take our rubbish,
the greed indulged,
the broken promises,
anger, resentments.

Take the long list of sin
that warps our being,
and weave your forgiving love
that makes of waste
a growing place.

Chris Polhill

The rich young ruler

A rich man asked Jesus: 'Good Teacher, what must I do to save the world?'

'Why do you call me good?' Jesus asked him. 'No one is good except God alone. You know what the sustainability manual says: Do not waste water or energy, shop thoughtfully and use the recycling facilities.'

The man replied: 'Ever since I was young I have lived in this way.'

When Jesus heard this, he said to him: 'There is still one more thing you must do – live so that nothing you do depletes the Earth's resources or does permanent damage to its habitat.' But when the man heard this he was sad because he had a comfortable life.

Jesus saw that he was sad and said: 'It is easier for a waste collection vehicle to enter the drive of a small council house, than for a rich man to live sustainably.'

John Polhill

Chip fat fuels lorries

A Norfolk haulage company runs its 45 lorries on bio-diesel and has not only saved thousands of pounds on fuel, but has been awarded contracts because of this environmentally friendly policy. It can do this because UCO (used cooking oil) collected from local supermarkets, restaurants and chip shops is processed by Global Commodities into 'driveECO bio-diesel'. The Customs and Excise, checking the lorries' emissions, said, 'The smoke coming from these exhaust systems is cleaner than the air we breathe.' Global Commodities, the UK's first and largest manufacturer of bio-diesel, began when a grandchild of the Norfolk entrepreneur Dennis Thouless said, 'Granddad, I think you've taken a lot out of this world. I think it's time you put something back in.'

Adapted from information from Global Commodities

Week five – shopping thoughtfully

One of the advantages of living in a free market economy is that we have choices about what we buy and how we buy it. What we often lack is information about how things are produced and a full understanding of the implications of a particular product choice (materials used, expected working life of the product, practicality of repair). By exercising informed choice we put pressure on producers to work in more environmentally conscious ways.

Actions

Choose two or three of these:

- Buy only what you need
- Repair and reuse rather than replace
- Check through the products you bought last year. How useful were they?
- Buy second-hand goods
- Make a list before you shop for food/household goods to avoid buying things you don't need
- Cook from primary ingredients (e.g. use fresh vegetables rather than processed food)
- Use the Mailing Preference Service to remove your name from junk mail lists
- Subscribe to a magazine like *Ethical Consumer*
- Eat vegetarian
- Eat vegan

Researching and campaigning

Choose one of these:

- Research the environmental behaviour/records of the companies you buy things from
- Write to your MP about improving labelling information on food and household goods

Calling for justice

Living God,
may we hear you calling for justice:
through the poor in a world of plenty;
through those oppressed by harsh regimes;
in the voices of the victims of religious legalism;
in the cries of the earth polluted by human greed;
in places where economics downgrade talent,
and efficiency outweighs care;
in the voices of the vulnerable in our hamlets and cities.

May the peace we seek
reflect your justice
and express your compassion and care.
Through Jesus, the Christ. Amen

Chris Polhill

Bless our choices

God bless this food,
locally grown,
produced in season.
God bless this food,
fairly traded,
giving new chances,
bringing new life.

Forgive our demands
for cheap food that costs the earth,
for cash crops from subsistence land,
for strawberries in December.

Forgive our ignorance
leading to hidden slaves,
dangerous conditions,
child labour.

God bless our choices
that, like lights in the open,
they may reveal your will, your kin-dom.

Chris Polhill

Living gently

Creator God, thank you for making so much:
for trees, stones and plants,
for their beauty and the life they give.
Bless us as we use them to make and build.
Help us to treasure these gifts of your providing
that we may live gently on earth
AND ALL CREATION PRAISE YOU.

Creator God, thank you for life-giving food:
for animals and fish, grain and plants,
for their beauty and the life they give.
Bless our care and use of them.
Help us to eat thankfully, and with due humility,
that we may live gently on earth
AND ALL CREATION PRAISE YOU.

Creator God, thank you for people:
for all their differences, their inventiveness,
and the ways they have fun.
Bless those who live in poverty and fear.
Help us to value each other
that we may live gently on earth
AND ALL CREATION PRAISE YOU.

Creator God, thank you for the choices we have,
the freedom we know, the joys we experience,
the purpose you give us.

Bless all our living on this planet you created.
Help us to be informed and to choose wisely
that we may live gently on earth
AND ALL CREATION PRAISE YOU.

And because we get confused about the best way
to live gently on earth;
and because we are caught in systems
that take a long time to change;
and because we cling to our way of life
and find it hard to change,

thank you for trusting us.
Thank you for Jesus beside us.
Thank you for the Holy Spirit giving us wisdom and strength.

HELP US TO LISTEN TO YOU
THAT WE MAY LIVE GENTLY ON EARTH
AND ALL CREATION PRAISE YOU.
AMEN

Chris Polhill

Supermarket psalm

A: Creator God, we praise you for the abundant variety of food here: twenty varieties – just of rice.

B: It's wonderful to see food from all over the world spread out on the supermarket shelves: food grown in many places.

A: But why is the fruit so uniform and clean? How many times has it been sprayed?

B: It worries me that small farmers suffer from supermarket demands; that they go out of business and cry for justice.

A: When I buy cheap food, how many workers do I dishonour? When I buy food from far away, how many workers have been cheated?

B: And there is so much packaging: the land will soon be full of rubbish, and remain unchanged for many generations.

A: There is so much there I fear the temptation to buy too much, to be greedy and only feasting.

B: Thank you for the growth of the Fairtrade movement and for organic food: practical justice for people and land.

A: Thank you for all the work behind the scenes: food from farms to shelves.

B: Help us to honour your creation in the way we shop, and to remember to take a reusable shopping bag.

Chris Polhill

Creation psalm

A: O God, I praise you for the joy creation brings to my heart: and the fascination you have given me to seek to understand and use new, gentler technologies.

B: I'm worried that everything I do seems to spoil the beauty of nature; that for every gain I make from technology there seems to be resultant damage to your precious creation.

A: I'm afraid that the economic drives of individuals and corporations will be stronger than the voices of those who want to follow a sustainable lifestyle, and that the consequences will be an irreversible environmental disaster.

B: Thank you for the freedom you give me to choose how I live: thank you for the model of living Jesus gives us.

A: Thank you for all people who care and campaign about environmental issues; thank you for scientists, business people and politicians who work to make sustainability more possible.

B: Help me to delight in letting creation be itself, to delight in the extra effort it takes to live sustainably, and to have a greater sense of your presence with me when I choose the gentler path.

John Polhill

The sea – a conversation

Voice of the sea

I am full of fine foods and beautiful treasures;
you may have them, you may see them.
I delight in providing for you.
Sustenance and beauty I give you,
O stewards, appointed by God.

Voice of commerce

I supply fish, 'The Big Dish';
the market demands seafood – high in protein, low in fat,
an abundant harvest there for the taking.
Faster efficient methods bring
first-rate produce at a reasonable price.
But it's not easy.
The profits are small:
insurance, equipment, boats, wages,
fishing grounds used by others,
and suddenly – fewer fish.
A short term problem, no doubt, but worrying …

Voice of the sea

You take too much!
I am rich and I am splendid,
but not infinitely so.
Curb your desires or I cannot nourish you.
Stop or both you and I will expire.

Voice of commerce

Wonderful place the sea, so deep, so vast,
our rubbish and sewage, in time, all recycled.
Amazing!
Fathomless depths
where we can safely leave nuclear waste till it is harmless;
waste which would otherwise contaminate the land.
And the sea provides cheap fuel
for our industry and homes.
Jobs for oil-riggers – prosperity for the country.
Just wonderful.

Voice of the sea

Allow me to breathe!
My lungs are full of poisons
and I die – and you with me.
The teeming life in me
succumbs to your excesses;
the treasures are tarnished and broken.
I hurt and weep.

From a creative writing workshop on Iona in 1998

Prayer of reconciliation

Lord, all living creatures are yours,
blessed by you.
Yet, we herd and pen them
as if we had created them.
They have no life
apart from our allowing.
Yet in spite of our 'efficiency'
many people are hungry.

Have mercy.

Lord, we pray for empathy
for your creatures' needs:
for community, companionship,
and freedom from distress.
Help us to pay heed to our call
to tend and nurture;
help us to co-operate with you
and be your image for them.
Amen

From a creative writing workshop on Iona in 1998

Look in our hearts, Lord Christ, we pray
(A call to economic faithfulness)

Look in our hearts, Lord Christ, we pray
And face us with what's true,
Who're tempted to deceive ourselves,
Accepting as our due
A disproportion of life's goods –
A wealth-distorted view.

You urged a straight and narrow way;
You call your folk to share,
Divest ourselves of Mammon's grip
And for our planet care:
But we persuade ourselves of wants
Which little leave to spare.

(continued)

Lord of St Francis, hound us still
That money lose its hold
Lest, in the end, not stigmata
Should mark our hands, but gold:
And we discern, as Judas did,
you were the one we sold.

Ian M Fraser/Donald Rennie (Tune: Ruth)

Week 6 – maintaining and increasing biodiversity

The song has a new verse: 'Where have all the sparrows gone, long time passing …' Fortunately there are many organisations actively promoting and working for species conservation and there is strong public support for this work. There are plenty of ways we can help, and it is often delightful and rewarding work.

Actions

Choose two or three of these:

– Don't drop any kind of litter (including cigarette ends) to avoid danger to wildlife
– Go litter picking
– Provide food for a variety of birds
– Visit a farm
– Put up bird and bat boxes
– Put up places for insects to hibernate in
– Drive slowly in the country and watch for animals
– Plant wild flowers and native species in your garden
– Leave wood piles to rot (habitat)
– Do not use weed killer or fertilisers on your lawn
– Have a meadow area in your garden (strimmer-cut once a year)
– Visit a local nature reserve
– Plant hedges
– Build a pond or bog garden

Research and campaigning

Choose one of these:

– Join a local conservation group
– Support farmers who manage for conservation
– Campaign for habitat creation in semi-public places (churchyards, play areas)
– Write to your MP about the need to control the use of genetically modified organisms

Weaver, thread and pattern

God, the Holy Trinity,
whose dance spins in chaotic order,
so grace our living as one and many
that we define ourselves
not by how we differ,
but by how we blend and weave
in the sparkle of your design.
So may our lives worship you,
weaver, thread and pattern. Amen

John Polhill

Litany for creation

The pain of the earth is raw,
like the pain of a mother
whose children are torn
from the softness and warmth of her breast.

The creatures of earth are torn
from the land
their ancestors roamed,
from the source of their health and renewal.

Humankind has been tearing the earth
and burning without limitation;
we consume the fruits of the fields,
pollute the rivers and streams.

And so creation is bound
in a terrible cycle of death
denying God's promise to each creature
held close to her heart

We must rise in the freedom we have,
repent of our failure to care,
restore a just balance to earth
by letting it teach us to love.

So might creation be healed
and God's heart be eased of its pain.

Yvonne Morland

Prayers of celebration and blessing

With mountains, hills and valleys;
With trees and all green-growing;
With oceans deep, rivers and sparkling streams;
WE PRAISE AND GLORIFY GOD, OUR CREATOR.

With swooping eagle and all birds of the air;
With lion and rabbit, and all that runs or crawls on land;
With leaping dolphins and all that swims in the waters;
WE PRAISE AND GLORIFY GOD, OUR CREATOR.

With all people, old and young;
With all races, short and tall;
With different faces – in all our wonderful difference and diversity;
WE PRAISE AND GLORIFY GOD, OUR CREATOR.

With all creation, we praise God
by being as we were made to be.
AMEN

We pray for those who work to care for creation:
those preserving forests and oceans,
Friends of the Earth, Greenpeace,
The Royal Society for the Protection of Birds, The Royal Society
for the Protection of Animals, Christian Ecology Link …
GOD BLESS THEM AND ENABLE THEM.

We pray for those who daily choose to work with or abuse creation:
Planners and developers,
farmers and fisher folk,
industrialists and bankers,
all who travel by land, sea or sky.
GOD BLESS THEM AND ENABLE THEM.

We pray for ourselves, for the choices we make daily:
what we buy,
how we travel,
what we reuse or recycle.

In all our struggles to live within God's harmony,
GOD BLESS US AND ENABLE US
THAT OUR LIVES MAY SING YOUR PRAISES.
AMEN

Chris Polhill

God made them

A: We believe God made the heavens and the earth.
B: Waters, sky and land; plants, trees and seeds.
     GOD MADE THEM AND LOVED THEM, AND SAW THAT THEY WERE GOOD.

A: We believe God created light and dark.
B: Sun, moon and stars; bright day and restful night.
     GOD MADE THEM AND LOVED THEM, AND SAW THAT THEY WERE GOOD.

A: We believe God made all creatures.
B: Bird, fish and animal; human beings in God's image.
     GOD MADE THEM AND LOVED THEM, AND SAW THAT THEY WERE GOOD.

A: Praise God, the Maker.
B: Praise God, the Son.
     PRAISE THE HOLY SPIRIT.
     GOD, THE THREE-IN-ONE.

Chris Polhill

Credo

I believe in a power beyond my imagination
that designed and put into force all the laws that govern the universe.
Laws that sometimes differ from my meagre attempts to understand or accept them.

I believe in a power that loves every part of creation.
A love that treats every wonderful, minute aspect of creation in the same way,
because of its unique place and contribution to the whole.

I believe in a power so secure in its own being
that it can allow me and others
the complete freedom to live and make plans and decisions.
Plans that may not always accord with the original design.
Decisions that bring destruction and pain
as well as growth and joy.

Bob Green

Creator of space and the mustard seed (a psalm)

A: Wonderful Creator, who dreamt a universe into being: who imagined the emptiness of space and the teeming life of the jungle.

B: We thank you for twig and tangle; we praise you for parabola and parasite.

A: When an egg hatches, your life breaks through; when a deer grazes, your peace lies on the grass.

B: But, Creator God, your creatures are dying: every year more species vanish that will never return.

A: People tear down great tracts of forest: they destroy complex habitats that they cannot restore.

B: Our seas are polluted and the fish have been taken; rain washes the soil from naked land and swollen rivers flood the land of the poor.

A: We fear the consequences of our actions; we try to convince ourselves that they are not as bad as we fear.

B: We don't want to forgo the lifestyle we enjoy; we don't want to make sacrifices when others do not.

A: We are frustrated because we are not free to live thoughtless lives; sad, because it feels as if the party is over.

B: We look at the scale of the universe and know that we are nothing: fiery suns and planets lie beyond our sight and understanding.

A: Yet we sense your care for the smallest bird; your touch on the most delicate flower.

B: Creator God of space and the mustard seed, we dare to be your hands: Good Maker of our hearts and spirits, we love to love your world.

John Polhill

Agricultural biodiversity in India
(Story from ITDG)

Orissa was once the home of the largest number of rice varieties of any state in India, more than 1,750. Now the number of local rice varieties is only approximately 150.

The tribal communities of Koraput district have used their knowledge and experience of forest species and agro-biodiversity to revitalise on-farm conservation by promoting traditional varieties of rice and medicinal plants. Community seed banks have ensured the preservation of biodiversity and food security, enabling communities to obtain, store and manage vital seed. Neighbouring villages have begun copying these practices for themselves; and many non-governmental organisations from surrounding districts have adopted seed and grain banking and community medicinal plant gardens to enhance the local biodiversity.

Adapted from *Hands On Gene Savers*

Western corporations limit biodiversity – check for local varieties of apples in your neighbourhood supermarket.

Research and campaigning sources on the Internet

Friends of the Earth is an international organisation and a good source of information on environmental issues and action. Friends of the Earth has a set of free leaflets covering the subjects on which it campaigns (available for the cost of postage only) and also publishes a number of books that cover most of the subjects in the Lent discipline:

Cutting Your Car Use
The Energy Saving House
Creative Sustainable Gardening
The Good Wood Guide
The Good Shopping Guide
Don't Throw It Away

Type in www.foei.org and from there link to your own country

Other internet sites

For transport, search 'Environmental transport' plus (+) your country's name

For the UK, the Environmental Transport Association campaigns on transport and other green issues and publishes a magazine for members. www.eta.co.uk

For the Walking Bus Movement: www.walkingbus.com

For water, try your water supplier or Search 'Water consumption' plus your country's name

For rain water harvesting: www.savetheenvironment.com

For the UK and domestic rain water harvesting: www.greenshop.co.uk

www.ecen.org gives European links for Christian ecology. For other countries type 'Christian Ecology' plus your country's name into the search engine.

Your government will have an agricultural statistics source; search the main governmental site.

For statistics about UK environmental issues visit the DEFRA website www.defra.gov.uk/environment/statistics. Also worth visiting is www.sustainable-development.gov.uk/indicators

For ethical shopping: *The Ethical Consumer* magazine www.ethicalconsumer.org

Campaigning information and information about companies can be found on www.corporatewatch.org.uk

For authoritative information about climate change from a reasonably neutral stand-point try www.newscientist.com/hottopics/climate

For more information about the Intermediate Technology Development Group (ITDG) visit their website: www.itdg.org or write to The Schumacher Centre for Technology and Development, Bourton Hall, Bourton-on-Dunsmore, Rugby CV23 9QZ, UK

For alternative technology: www.peopleinaction.info/alternativetechnology/

In the UK, www.cat.org.uk is worth visiting and has a good range of literature on green issues.

Biodiversity subjects are covered well by societies protecting bird life. Search 'Society+protection+bird' to find an organisation relevant to your own country.

For the Royal Society for the Protection of Birds: www.rspb.org.uk

For the World Wildlife Foundation: www.wwf.org

Global Action Plan is also worth visiting. www.globalactionplan.org.uk

www.myfootprint.org has a questionnaire that helps you to assess the amount of the earth's surface your household uses to sustain its lifestyle.

Greenpeace is also worth visiting. www.greenpeace.org

To stop junk mail try 'Mailing Preference Service'.
In the UK, register to be excluded from mailing lists on www.mpsonline.org.uk

Opening and closing responses for Sundays in Lent

(Where denominational lectionaries differ, some alternative readings and responses are included.)

1st Sunday of Lent

Cycle A
Gen 2:7–9, 3:1–7; Ps 51; Rom 5:12–19; Mt 4:1–11

Creator God
Walking in the garden
BREATHE LIFE INTO US

Tempted God
Praying in the desert
BREATHE LIFE INTO US

Holy God
Travelling towards the city
BREATHE LIFE INTO US

> Mysterious God
> Maker and encourager
> SURPRISE US WITH ANGELS

> Revealing God
> Questioner and caller
> SURPRISE US WITH STORIES

> Breathing God
> Dancer and delighter
> SURPRISE US WITH JOY

Cycle B
Gen 9:8–15; Ps 25; 1 Pet 3:18–22; Mk1:12–15

Round about us
Here among us
GOD OF PROMISE AND LOVE

Good and faithful
Strong in mercy
GOD OF PROMISE AND LOVE

Calling our names
Bidding us welcome
GOD OF PROMISE AND LOVE

> God is among us
> SHOUT THE GOOD NEWS

> God is ahead of us
> TRUST THE GOOD NEWS

> God is within us
> LIVE THE GOOD NEWS

Cycle C
Deut 26:4–10; Ps 91; Rom10:8–13; Lk 4:1–13

Wanderers, gatherers,
Homemakers, travellers
WE COME TO GOD

Questioners, adventurers,
Believers, doubters,
WE COME TO GOD

Workers, menders
Seekers, dreamers,
WE COME TO GOD

> Wherever we travel
> GOD IS ON OUR TRACK

> Wherever we settle
> GOD IS IN OUR MIDST

> Whatever is ahead of us
> GOD WILL BE THERE BEFORE US

> God's angels are among us
> TO KEEP US IN ALL OUR WAYS

2nd Sunday of Lent

Cycle A
Gen 12:1–4; Ps 33; 2 Tim1:8–10; Mt 17:1–19

Gathering God
Our rock and shelter
WE ARE HERE TO MEET WITH YOU

Travelling God
Our way and wonder
WE ARE HERE TO MEET WITH YOU

Summoning God
Our joy and adventure
WE ARE HERE TO MEET WITH YOU

> From what we know
> To what we have yet to discover
> GOD IS CALLING US ON

> From all that binds us
> To the truth which frees us
> GOD IS CALLING US ON

> From the blessings of today
> To the possibilities of tomorrow
> GOD IS CALLING US ON

Alternative:

Cycle A
Gen 12:1–4; Ps 121; Rom 4:1–5,13–17; John 3:1–17

God watches over
Our waking and sleeping
OUR HELP COMES FROM GOD
WHO MADE HEAVEN AND EARTH

God saves our feet
From slipping and stumbling
OUR HELP COMES FROM GOD
WHO MADE HEAVEN AND EARTH

God keeps guard
Over our comings and goings
OUR HELP COMES FROM GOD
WHO MADE HEAVEN AND EARTH

> Adventurous God
> Travelling lightly
> BREATHE IN US

> Courageous God
> Confronting injustice
> BREATHE IN US

> Mysterious God
> Blowing wildly
> BREATHE IN US

> Pilgrim God
> Light in our darkness
> BREATHE IN US
> ALL OUR NIGHTS AND DAYS

Cycle B
Gen 22:1–2, 9–13,15–18; Ps 116; Rom 8:31–34; Mk 9:2–10

When we are happy
When we are full of sadness
GOD WELCOMES US WITH LOVE

When we are bewildered
When we are full of questions
GOD WELCOMES US WITH LOVE

When we are joyful
When we are full of wonder
GOD WELCOMES US WITH LOVE

Strong and mysterious
Bright and holy
GOD IS ON THE SIDE OF LOVE

Wise and questioning
Just and joyful
GOD IS ON THE SIDE OF TRUTH

Wild and challenging
Glorious and graceful
GOD IS ON THE SIDE OF HOPE

Alternative:

Cycle B
Gen 17:1–7,15–16; Ps 22:23–31; Rom 4:13–25; Mk 8:31–38

When Abraham chuckled
and Sarah laughed
GOD PROMISED THEM LIFE

When Abraham wondered
and Sarah hoped
GOD PROMISED THEM JOY

We tell the story
of God's love and laughter
WE REJOICE IN THE PROMISES OF GOD

Jesus calls us
To leave the past
JESUS CALLS US TO HOPE

Jesus calls us
To travel lightly
JESUS CALLS US TO FAITH

Jesus calls us
To live fairly
JESUS CALLS US TO JUSTICE

Jesus calls us
To risky living
JESUS CALLS US TO LIFE

Cycle C
Gen 15:5–12, 17–18; Ps 27; Phil 3:17–4:1; Lk 9:28–36

Our homeland is on earth
Our homeland is in heaven
WE ARE PEOPLE OF GOD

Our lives are commonplace
Our lives are full of wonder
WE ARE PEOPLE OF GOD

Our song is of love and hope
Our life in God is eternal
WE ARE PEOPLE OF GOD

    Hold firm, take heart
    God is our stronghold
    WE ARE NOT ALONE

    Be brave, be holy
    God is our justice
    WE ARE NOT ALONE

    Be amazed, be joyful
    God is our glory
    WE ARE NOT ALONE

Alternative:

Cycle C

Gen 15:1–12,17–18; Ps 27; Phil 3:17–4:1; Lk 13:31–35

Secure on a rock
You gather us
YOU WRAP US ROUND IN LOVE

Under your wings
You gather us
YOU WRAP US ROUND IN LOVE

Safe in your house
You gather us
YOU WRAP US ROUND IN LOVE

> In the goodness of God
> WE ARE TRAVELLING HOME

> In the justice of Jesus
> WE ARE TRAVELLING HOME

> In the song of the Spirit
> WE ARE TRAVELLING HOME

3rd Sunday of Lent

Cycle A

Ex 17:3–7; Ps 95; Rom 5:1–2, 5–8; Jn 4:5–42

Pilgrim God
Striking water in the desert
REFRESH US AND QUENCH OUR THIRST

Revealing God
Sitting by the well side
REFRESH US AND TEACH US TRUTH

Dancing God
Moving over the waters
REFRESH US AND BRING US LIFE

We are God's people
Loved and cherished
WE GO OUT IN JOY

We are God's people
Called and challenged
WE GO OUT IN JOY

We are God's people
Refreshed and forgiven
WE GO OUT IN JOY

Cycle B
Ex 20:1–17; Ps 19; 1 Cor 1:22–25; Jn 2:13–25

Wise God
Jealous and holy
YOUR LOVE BRINGS US TRUTH

Wise God
Just and joyful
YOUR STORIES BRING US HOPE

Wise God
Wakeful and surprising
YOUR BREATH BRINGS US LIFE

Teach us truth
Gladden our hearts
CIRCLE US WITH LOVE

Trust us with justice
Sweeten our days
CIRCLE US WITH LOVE

Keep us holy
Give light to our eyes
CIRCLE US WITH LOVE

Cycle C
Ex 3:1–8,13–15; Ps 103; 1 Cor 10:1–6,10–12; Lk 13:1–9

Blazing in a bush
Burning in a fiery pillar
Moses met you
COME GOD AND MEET US NOW

Walking through a city
Listening to a story
Disciples met you
COME GOD AND MEET US NOW

Fire round their heads
Holiness in their lives
Believers met you
COME GOD AND MEET US NOW

> Holy God
> Rich in mercy
> BLESS US WITH LOVE

> Healing God
> Firm in forgiveness
> BLESS US WITH GRACE

> Disturbing God
> Strong in justice
> BLESS US WITH HOPE AND JOY

4th Sunday of Lent

Cycle A
1 Sam 16:1,6–7,10–13; Ps 23; Eph 5:8–14; Jn 9:1–41

God of darkness and light
OPEN OUR EYES TO YOUR JUSTICE

God of goodness and glory
OPEN OUR MINDS TO YOUR WISDOM

God of mercy and kindness
OPEN OUR HEARTS TO YOUR LOVE

> Shield us God
> with your crook
> and your staff
> BRING US SAFELY HOME

> Guide us God
> with your truth
> and your goodness
> BRING US SAFELY HOME

> Encourage us God
> with your oil
> and your kindness
> BRING US SAFELY HOME

> Shepherd us God
> walk with us
> always
> BRING US SAFELY HOME

Cycle B
2 Chron 36:14–16,19–23; Ps 137; Eph 2:4–10; Jn 3:14–21

God dances in light
God delights in creation
GOD LOVES THE WORLD

God made the world
And all that is in it
GOD LOVES THE WORLD

God saves us through grace
It is none of our doing
GOD LOVES THE WORLD

Shine in our lives
Warm us with courage
KEEP US CLOSE TO YOU

Shine in our lives
Light up our darkness
KEEP US CLOSE TO YOU

Shine in our lives
Sweeten our sadness
KEEP US CLOSE TO YOU

Shine in our lives
Raise us up to glory
KEEP US CLOSE TO YOU

Cycle C
1 Josh 5:9–12; Ps 34; 2 Cor 5:17–21; Lk 15:1–3,11–32

Young and old
Friends and strangers
GOD WELCOMES US

Lost and bewildered
Found and rejoicing
GOD WELCOMES US

Proud of our success
Afraid of our poverty
GOD WELCOMES US

This morning, this day
This night, for ever
GOD WELCOMES US
WITH A HUG OF LOVE

Our message is this:
GOD WELCOMES SINNERS
AND EATS WITH THEM

Our hope is this:
GOD WELCOMES SINNERS
AND EATS WITH THEM

Our home is this:
GOD WELCOMES SINNERS
AND EATS WITH THEM

5th Sunday of Lent

Cycle A
Ezek 37:12–14; Ps 130; Rom 8:8–11; Jn 11:1–45

Loving God
Hear our cry
BRING US TO LIFE

Redeeming God
Rescue us
BRING US TO LIFE

Spirit of God
Breathe on us
BRING US TO LIFE

>The love of God
>is at home in us
>WE GO OUT IN PEACE

>The justice of Jesus
>is at home in us
>WE GO OUT IN HOPE

>The wildness of God's Spirit
>is at home in us
>WE GO OUT IN WONDER AND JOY

Cycle B
Jer 31:31–34; Ps 51; Heb 5:7–9; Jn 12:20–30

In winter
and springtime
In summer
and harvest
GOD SPEAKS TO US

In struggle
and suffering
In death
and resurrection
GOD SPEAKS TO US

In word
and action
In prayer
and promise
GOD SPEAKS TO US

> Holy God
> GIVE ME A HAPPY HEART
>
> Wise God
> GIVE ME A SEEKING MIND
>
> Strong God
> GIVE ME GENTLE HANDS
>
> Pilgrim God
> GIVE ME COURAGE AND JOY

Cycle C
Is 43:16–21; Ps 126; Phil 3:8–14; Jn 8:1–11

God of the past
God of our memories
WE ARE HERE TO THANK YOU

God of the future
God of our dreams
WE ARE HERE TO TRUST YOU

God of the present
God of our salvation
WE ARE HERE TO PRAISE YOU

You put songs on our lips
and make us your people
YOU DO GREAT THINGS FOR US
AND WE ARE GLAD

God on the road
God in the wilderness
GOD MAKING ALL THINGS NEW

God in our tears
God in our laughter
GOD MAKING ALL THINGS NEW

God in our living
God in our dying
GOD MAKING ALL THINGS NEW

Alternative:
Cycle C
Is 43:16–21; Ps 125; Phil 3:8–14; Jn 12:1–8

God of glory
At home in the universe
MAKE YOUR HOME IN US

Loving Jesus
At home in Bethany
MAKE YOUR HOME IN US

Holy Spirit
At home in humanity
MAKE YOUR HOME IN US

Holy God
KEEP OUR EYES ON THE PRIZE

Holy Jesus
KEEP OUR EYES ON THE PRIZE

Holy Spirit
KEEP OUR EYES ON THE PRIZE

The race is on
WE ARE RUNNING HOME TO GOD

Ruth Burgess

Mothering Sunday

Under your wings

How many times have I wanted to put my arms around all your people, just as a hen gathers her chicks under her wings, but you would not let me. (Luke 13:34)

Under your wings
You would hide us
MOTHERING GOD

Under your wings
You would shelter us
MOTHERING GOD

Under your wings
You would warm us
MOTHERING GOD

Under your wings
You would nurture us
MOTHERING GOD.

Ruth Burgess

You let us go

Mothering God
You watch your children grow
AND YOU LET US GO

Mothering God
You teach us what is true
AND YOU LET US GO

Mothering God
You show us what is just
AND YOU LET US GO

Mothering God
You give us what we need
AND YOU LET US GO

Ruth Burgess

Out of your womb

Out of your womb
into the light
YOU PUSH US IN LOVE

Out of childhood
into adult responsibility
YOU PUSH US IN LOVE

Out of dependence
into freedom and risk
YOU PUSH US IN LOVE

Ruth Burgess

When we cry

When we cry
you rock us
When we are hungry
you feed us
YOU LOVE US
MOTHERING GOD

When we are lost
you find us
When we are happy
you laugh with us
YOU LOVE US
MOTHERING GOD

As we grow
you respect us
When we leave home
you bless us
YOU LOVE US
MOTHERING GOD

Ruth Burgess

The image of God

Young mothers
Old mothers
Grandmothers
ALL MOTHERS ARE MADE
IN THE IMAGE OF GOD

Childless women
Menopausal women
Lesbian women
ALL WOMEN ARE MADE
IN THE IMAGE OF GOD

Fathers
Gay men
Childless men
ALL MEN ARE MADE
IN THE IMAGE OF GOD

Divorced people
Married people
Single people
ALL PEOPLE ARE MADE
IN THE IMAGE OF GOD

Ruth Burgess

A good enough parent

Father of God
protecting your son
against slander and danger
YOU WERE
A GOOD ENOUGH PARENT

Mother of God
losing your son
on the streets of Jerusalem

YOU WERE
A GOOD ENOUGH PARENT

Father God
letting your children
face pain and laughter
YOU ARE
A GOOD ENOUGH PARENT

Mother God
loving your children
through good and through evil
YOU ARE
A GOOD ENOUGH PARENT

Parenting God
father, mother, and holy spirit
HELP US TO TAKE
THE LOVING RISKS
OF PARENTHOOD.

Ruth Burgess

('Good-enough parenting', as compared to a perfect or idealised style of parenting.)

You father and mother us

Loving God,
you father us and mother us
all our days.
Even before we acknowledged you
you loved us;
you laboured to bring us to birth,
new birth,
and how joyful for you was that birthing.
In the secret places of our lives
you nourish us,
offering us the feeding
that we need
to grow as human beings.

No matter how often
we desert you
you never turn your face away from us,
and your abiding concern
is always for our good.
You weep for us,
you laugh with us,
you rejoice in our successes
and are in anguish at our pain.

Yours are the arms
reaching out to cradle us
when we collapse in death.

Loving, mothering God,
strong and tender,
tried and true,
we worship you today.

John Harvey

The pictures of you in our minds

Loving God,
forgive us,
how we have got you wrong!
Lazily we have settled for pictures of you in our minds
which tell a terrible tale.
We have painted you
stern and unbending,
the eternal judge
with no mercy, no compassion.
We have summoned you
onto our side
in battle –
in boardroom or in war –

giving you a uniform to wear
of our own making.
Too often
we have been responsible
for turning others away from you,
and, in the end,
from turning away from you ourselves.
Forgive us
and lead us into the truth
of your full nature
as shown in Jesus.

John Harvey

Come, Mother God

Come, Mother God:
come as an enfolding nurturing presence,
come as steadfast love
to hold us.

Come, Father God:
come as an enabling, strengthening force,
come as tough love
to let us go.

Come, Parent God:
come as friend and comforter
healing our wounds,
walking our way.

Come as wounded healer
to make us whole.

John Harvey

With deep gratitude

Lord God,
father and mother of us all,
hear us as we give thanks
for mothers, and for mothering,
on this special day.

We remember before you
with deep gratitude
our own mothers.

We also give thanks
for all in our immediate family
and in our wide circle of friends and relatives,
both women and men,
who shared in our nurturing and growth.

Look with love and mercy,
we pray,
on all the very mixed emotions
that run through us today.

Hallow our memories,
forgive our guilt or shame,
and enable us
to be at peace with our feelings and thoughts.

John Harvey

Hear our prayers

Hear our prayers
for all mothers today.

We pray for the mothers and grandmothers among us.
We pray for all expectant mothers,

and for those who would wish to bear children
but who cannot.

We pray for mothers with no experience,
or bad experience,
of being mothered themselves.

We pray for single mothers,
for whom being a mother is sometimes a nightmare.

We pray especially for mothers
who are forced to watch while their children starve
or suffer
or grow sick.

We remember before you
mothers whose children have been killed –
in road accidents,
in house fires,
or by troubled human beings.
And we remember still
the mothers of Dunblane in Scotland …

Lastly,
we remember with love
those grieving the deaths of their mothers in recent days …
Let your mothering love surround them at this time
and bring them comfort and strength.

John Harvey

Family

Part one

You weren't sure, were you Joseph?
He looked like the others,
but you'd been told that he wasn't yours.
Bethlehem and Egypt were over now.
The running had stopped,
but so had the angels.
You were home in Nazareth,
back with your friends,
immersed in your work.
And your family had grown.
But the first-born,
he looked more like you than
anyone else in the village;
but you weren't sure.

Part two

You watched him as he grew,
didn't you Mary?
Was he going to be so holy, so different,
that you wouldn't be able to cope?
He was soon walking,
running into the arms of whoever
would catch him.
And when he neared speech,
you made sure that the first word he said was daddy –
Abba – and that was for Joseph
not for God.
He made friends easily.
He was good with his brothers and sisters,
bed time stories a speciality.
'Tell us another one, Jesus!'
He learnt his trade from Joseph,
his letters from the rabbi,
his first prayers from you.
Weekly he shared in the Sabbath meals,

as the youngest child,
he asked the Passover questions: 'Why?'
Sometimes he went with you to Jerusalem,
and you watched him Mary.
He wasn't a loner like John, his cousin.
He seemed to be growing up normal and strong.

Part three

Three days!
In the first hours he could have been
dead on the Jericho road.
He could have been kidnapped,
beaten, or worse.
They retraced their steps.
They asked everyone they met. Nothing.

In the city there was nowhere else to look.
All they could do now was to commit him to God
and take the other children home.

So they went to the temple to speak their prayer.
And there they saw him –
sitting
talking,
alive,
unharmed.
They couldn't believe it.
'Jesus – why have you done this to us?
For three days we've been looking for you.
We thought you were dead!'
'Why Jesus – where have you been?
Son, I want to wallop you and
hug you at the same time.'
And the why was returned.
'Why didn't you know where to find me?
Why didn't you know I'd be
in my Abba's house?'
They looked at each other then,
Jesus and Joseph and Mary,

their eyes meeting,
love and pain mingling in their questions,
receiving no answers they could understand.

Part four

So what happened in those years, Jesus?
Did you begin to wonder who you were?
Did Mary tell you about the angel, the massacre?
Did Joseph tell you about the shepherds, about Egypt, about his fears?

If they didn't, someone in the village must have told you about the census,
must have let slip that your family
went missing for a few years and then reappeared.

You didn't think like your parents, did you Jesus?
They couldn't answer your questions – that worried them;
and you wondered if they were refusing to answer you.
What did they know about you that they wouldn't tell?

Did you continue to talk with the teachers in Jerusalem year after year?
Did you want to join them?
Were your parents over-protective, or did they let you do your own thing?
Was there enough work for you to stay in the family business?
Did you go out with your friends? Did you have a girlfriend?
Could you relax in the village or did you feel a stranger?

And of God – what did you know?
Did you know as much as your growing mind could take?
Were you able to believe it? Who could you talk to?
Who would believe you? Who might laugh at you?
Who might threaten you?

Adolescence is full of questions –
of mind and body and emotions out of gear –
why for you should it have been any different?
And, in the end, did you know who you were –
or what was going to happen to you?
Or did you, like us,
have to live your life and see what happened next?

Ruth Burgess

Additional liturgical resources for Lent

Plumb line prayer

Then God said, 'See, I am setting a plumb line in the midst of my people.'(Amos 7:8)

God of justice, mercy and truth,
we gather in your presence,
aware of it in all creation –
where the warmth of the sun, the strength of the wind,
the energy of the waves, the stability of the earth
all remind us of your constant love
and your power to change and challenge our lives.

God of justice, mercy and truth,
we gather in your presence,
aware that in our world
there is one law for the rich and one for the poor,
that the scales are weighted against many
of our sisters and brothers,
and against new nations struggling to become,
and to find a balance.

God of justice, mercy and truth,
we gather in your presence,
aware of our own lives –
individually and in community –
where they measure up,
where they fall short,
where they are out of kilter –
as your plumb line shows us what is true.

Help us to be true to ourselves,
true to our history,
true to our own story,
true to you. AMEN

Jan Sutch Pickard

Not a good day

I know you are angry, says God.
Your silence screams.
So get real,
be your hidden self with me;
the one that is not nice,
not nice at all.

Don't be embarrassed,
bawl if you want to.
Rage.
Sulk.
Kick and pout like a child;
I like children.
Yes, poo, tantrums and all, since you ask.
So when someone says, 'Let us pray …'
Knot your arms and mutter,
'Shan't!'
If it helps,
it's where you are just now.
And where you are is
exactly where I want to be too.
With you.

Frances Copsey

A statement of faith

We believe in God,
who made the sun and the sky, the stars and the sea,
who calls us to live responsibly.

We believe in Jesus Christ,
who became human
who healed the sick
who talked to children
who made friends with sinners.
He burned brightly and offended many.

His journey was one of life and death and resurrection.
His light continues to shine in darkness.

We believe in the Holy Spirit,
who inspires the scriptures
and whose breath we breathe.

We believe that God calls us to be a community,
committed to one another
offering a welcome to everyone
old and young
rich and poor
strong and weak.

We believe that God calls us to be peacemakers
workers for justice
brothers and sisters
a light for our world. Amen

Written by two fourteen-year-old boys at a worship workshop on Iona

Searching

Not in the sky
the stars
Not in the fingers of frost
or a leaf
or a sunbeam
Not in all their beauty
and beauty it surely is
can I ever prove you, God.

In a friend's smile
a child's laugh
an old man's tears
I get nearer
but never near enough.

Ah God,
can I ever know –

ever be sure?
I think not.

Prayer, ideas, words,
these help to draw you closer;
it isn't with the unreal
that I talk in the darkness
and walk in the light.

I jumped – and landed
in your country
your way of seeing
of touching
a long time back;
and despite the mind's questioning
I am still here
found
and yet still searching.

Ruth Burgess

Credo

Theologically speaking I'm one of the awkward squad,
always asking questions
or questioning answers;
it's uncomfortable for all concerned,
especially me.
I wish it wasn't so;
wish I could tuck myself up in tradition,
snuggle down into certainty,
learn to trust,
but I don't know how –
don't even know what the God-word means to me now.
I do know love when I meet it though.
Oh yes, I recognise Love.

Frances Copsey

A bit of hope – Lent 2004

Dreadful, dreadful injustice is being carried out in our world and I along with most people feel hopeless. Linsey, from my slimming club, thought my STOP BUSH badge was something to do with leg waxing. My County-Durham mother-in-law was so offended by the badge that I was asked to remove it before visiting elderly relatives.

George Bush ('Junior' to his friends) was a good man, it seems, because he ate fish and chips at the 'Dun Cow', and said grace before he ate. He is a very religious man, unlike Osama Bin Laden.

The injustice of life surrounds us, from religious intolerance to natural disasters to smocks. (Although I have had to concede, after a lot of telephone canvassing, that cerise smocks have a certain something!)

Brian, a new client, swanned into the soup kitchen with a cigarette (Satan's chimney) and brimmed up with bravado. As usual, we started the main course with a prayer.

In the second's silence before I began, Brian screamed: 'You are offering people false hope, this is a pack of lies.'

During my year as soup kitchen co-ordinator nobody had dared to shout out before. There was silence. If the teaspoons hadn't all been stolen you could have heard them drop.

'What on earth can God do for us? It is only rich people who go to church. Give us all a million pounds and I will believe in God,' Brian demanded.

I gazed around my gathered flock. Everyone was open-mouthed and staring, apart from Dock, who was asleep on a wheaten roll.

I said in a Miss Jean Brodie voice: 'Do you believe wealth would make you happy?'

And Brian answered very suitably: 'It's only you rich bastards who believe in God. Did God give you all your money?'

I went into a long discourse about Jesus, born in a barn, refugee parents, a traveller dependent on the hospitality of others.

Brian banged his plastic fork on the table: 'He had a nice life!'

I continued: 'He died a horrible death, fighting for breath, abandoned by friends, destitute, killed as a criminal.'

Brian's face changed. He looked not moved, only powerless.

Brian shouted: 'F*** off.'

Bella said: 'Will I kick him in?'

'No Bella, leave him,' I said, bringing justice to a hopeless man.

Brian, knowing dear Bella's reputation, looked relieved.

Bella, an ex–heroin addict recently reinstated on the caravan site, shouted: 'Listen son, this place gives me hope, and you need a bit of hope. We all need a bit of hope.'

Dock woke up: 'Are there any cakes tonight?' And the real work of justice began.

Louise Glen-Lee

It's us again

Prayer of approach

Here we are; it's us again –
bothering you, and wondering
if we would want to be bothered.

Yet here we are, too late to turn back,
ground down by evil, lifted up by hope,
and reaching out
for more than we see, hear, conceive or imagine.

Prayer of confession

Sorry about last week.
Things got on top of me.

I walked on by; turned up the volume.

Left you to get on with
what was mine to do.

All right,
never mind the accidents and the failures,
let's do a deal:
Sorry for the things that I knew were wrong,
alone or in company,
but went ahead and did
or left undone.

Silence

God, if anyone can cope with us you can.
Here is all the stuff that weighs us down –
you won't look the other way.
But take it off our hands.
Set us free. Forgive us.

And show us, here and now,
the people you know we can be.

GLORY TO YOU
THROUGH ALL YOU SHAPE AND LOVE.
PEACE TO EVERY CREATURE. AMEN

David Coleman

Gracious and patient God

Gracious and patient God – we hope!
There are times when you must feel
that we were sent to try you
with our prejudice, our apathy, our intransigence,
and our refusal to receive the grace
that we are made whole by the cross of our Lord.

Forgive all our ingratitude, our small-mindedness, our stiff necks,
and bind up our brokenness.
We are without excuse,
but bold to ask pardon
from our Lord who lived his life
and died his death
and gave his flesh and blood
for the forgiveness of our sins.
Let us share silence
and consider where we have gone wrong …

David Coleman

Lead us on our journey

God, our God,
you have called us to be a people
on the move;
travelling light,
dying to live,
ready to lose ourselves for the sake of the world.

You have called us to be a people
with a purpose;
travelling without a map,
travelling to where we are led,
sustained by your Spirit,
committed to the gospel for the hope of the world.

You have called us, your people,
to be the church.
But we are a church with problems:
too strong for the weak,
too staid for the young,
too respectable for the poor,
too divided for mission,
too obsessed with our own lives to think of the lives of others,
too unsure of our message to speak to the world.

Move us on our journey
from where we are to where you want us to go.
Open our eyes on the way
to the people of different cultures, continents and countries,
who can bring colour to our lives.

Take us on our journey
from where we are to what you want us to be;
so that we become a community
where all are welcomed and no one is excluded,
all are valued and no one is made to feel inadequate,
all are forgiven and no one is ashamed to belong,
all are encouraged and no one is too hurt to come among us.

Lead us on our journey
from who we are to who you want us to be;
so that patience is built into us,
kindness is assumed in us,
gentleness is part of us,
compassion flows from us,
truth is second nature to us,
and the commitment of love is part of us.

Let us go gladly on the journey towards Easter –
the journey towards death and resurrection.
Let us journey in the peace and power of the Spirit.

Ruth Harvey

A pilgrim people

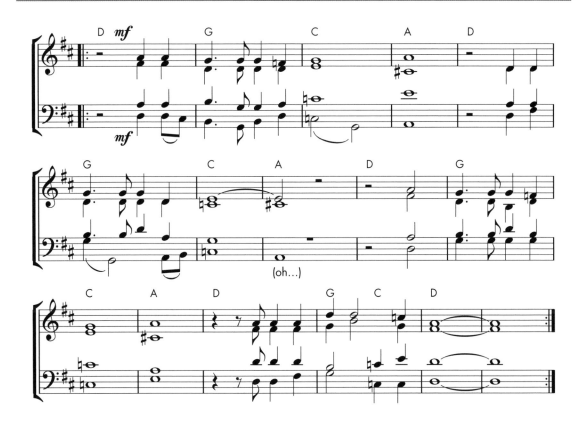

God be with us on our journey.
Jesus, guide us in your love.
Lord, gift us through each other –
a pilgrim people renew.

da Noust

Broken

1. Bro - ken,   all of us bro - ken.   All of us loved,____ all of us

loved.   Cho - sen,   each of us cho - sen.

In -vit -ed to life,   in - vit -ed to life.

2. All   you   make_ our God   is   good,   you fash -ion   old____ in -to

new._____   All   you   make____ our God   is

good,_   you   free   our   hearts__ with   your   love._____

3. Tra - vel,   each of us tra - vel,   Com -pan -ions to -

- ge - ther_____   walk -ing   the   way.

Beau - ty,   dis -cov -er -ing beau - ty.   Light -ing the

dark - ness,   sur - pris -ing   us   all.   *repeat verses 2 and 1*

Tenor (sung from verse 3)

3. Tra - vel,   each of us tra - vel,   Com - pan - ions to -

- ge - ther_____ walk - ing the way.

Beau - ty,   dis - cov - er - ing beau - ty.   Light - ing the

dark - ness,   sur - pris - ing us all.

2. All you make__ our God is good,__ you fash - ion old__ in - to

new._____ All you make__ our God is

good,__ you free our hearts__ with your love._____

1. Bro - ken,   all of us bro - ken.   All of us loved,_____ all of us

loved.   Cho - sen,   each of us cho - sen.

In - vit - ed to life,   in - vit - ed to life.

John Coleman

The quiet insistence of your Word

What I notice most about this place
is the wind, veering and backing
into my corner, eddying,
gusting, niggling,
tangling hair, finding the contours of my face
with icy fingers.

Yesterday I had a place in the sun.
It's easy to pray with silences,
warm light, and seabirds calling.

Today is hard. I pull my collar up,
and draw my fingers, monk-like,
into my sleeves. The wind
buffets my ears, so I no longer
hear your voice in the song of the lark,
the flutter of small birds.

Lord, do not let this northeast wind,
or any other, deafen me
to the still, small voice,
the quiet insistence of your Word.

Alma Hamilton

Resurrecting

The sun
warms my back
while the black
earth in my hand
carries the memory
of winter's
icy
iron grip.
Frost
fingers
spring's
first bold beginnings
threateningly,
but
the budding of trees
betrays
nature's
secret
understanding
of death and resurrection.

This is a good time for me,
between snowdrop and daffodil;
I would wish
perhaps
to spend
eternity
here
on the threshold of things –
expectant.

Nevertheless,
even here,
I grope for meaning
(instead of simply being);
resurrection,
salvation,
redemption,

each
suggest to me
a process
rather than
a condition,
an ebb
and flow,
a signpost
rather than
a destination.

For now
it is sufficient
to have caught
a glimpse
of that possibility.

This time,
between snowdrop
and daffodil,
encourages me
to wait.

Pete Anderson

God hears all kinds of prayers
(A reflection on Luke 18:9–14)

Readers: Narrator, Pharisee, Tax Collector, Man, Woman

Narrator: God hears all kinds of prayers …

Once there were two men who went up to the Temple to pray: one was a Pharisee, the other a tax collector.

The Pharisee stood apart by himself and prayed.

Pharisee: I thank you God that I am not like everyone else:
                   I am not greedy,

I am not dishonest,
I am not an adulterer.
I thank you God that I am not like that tax collector over there.
I keep your laws,
I fast two days a week,
I give you a tenth of my income.

Narrator: The tax collector stood at the back of the temple, far away from the Pharisee. He was afraid to raise his face to heaven so he looked at the floor and beat his breast and cried.

Tax Collector: God, have pity on me a sinner.

Narrator: God hears all kinds of prayers.

    (Pause)

Narrator: Once there were two people, a man and a woman, who went into a cathedral to pray. The man walked slowly up the middle aisle, admiring the stained glass windows and the polished pews. Giving an approving glance at the Christian Aid display in the side chapel, he settled himself down in the front pew and, after a few moments, began to pray.

Man: Thank you God for this beautiful cathedral, I really appreciate it.
I love coming in here to pray.
You know me, God,
I do my best to live a responsible life. I have a good job.
I am not in debt and I fill in my tax returns correctly and on time.
I have a good wife.
I am faithful to her and I make sure that she and the children are well cared for and are a credit to me.
Whenever possible we eat fairly traded food and we drink fairly traded coffee.
It tastes a lot better than it used to …
I am willing to give money to good causes –
as long as I have satisfied myself that my money is being put to a good use
and is not being squandered.
Anything we no longer need and all our unwanted Christmas presents are taken to the Oxfam shop in the next town.

Narrator: The woman crept into the back of the cathedral and sat down in a side pew, sheltered by a pillar. Her eyes were full of tears. Her day was not going well. The debt collectors had arrived early demanding money, her boyfriend had stormed out of the house saying that he had had enough and he wasn't coming back, and her children would be home from school soon and she'd promised them money tomorrow so that they could go on the school trip next week. She'd not been able to face going into work today, but she'd have to go in tomorrow or she'd lose her job.

She'd not prayed for a long time, but she needed help and maybe God might hear her; so she buried her head in her arms and prayed …

Woman: Help me, God.
I'm sorry, God.
Please, God, help me …

Narrator: God hears all kinds of prayers …

And God says:
Those who think themselves important will be welcomed and humbled; and those who face the truth about themselves will be welcomed and helped.

(5-minute conversation with a neighbour. Ask each other these questions: 'What is your imagined picture of a Pharisee or a tax collector? What reinforces the Pharisee in you?'[2] Share your thoughts and feelings.)

Narrator: For the Word of God in scripture,
for the Word of God among us,
for the Word of God within us,
ALL: THANKS BE TO GOD.

Ruth Burgess

Gladly we pray

Glad-ly we pray,   glad-ly we praise,   glad-ly to God our   long-ings raise;

sure of God's love,   need-ing God's grace,   meet-ing__ God face to   face.

Gladly we pray,
Gladly we praise,
Gladly to God
Our longings raise;
Sure of God's love,
Needing God's grace,
Meeting God face to face.

Prayer is a gate,
On it we swing
Sometimes, our thoughts
Just wandering;
But when we need
Heart for the road
Prayer opens wide to God.

Hear, then, our praise,
Heed then our prayer,
Lord of the here
And everywhere:
We put our lives
Where they belong:
You are our hope and song!

Ian M Fraser/Donald Rennie (Tune: Hear us)

The tune Southgate (Watts) could also be used with these words.

O God, you are my God (Psalm 63)

O God, you are my God, for you I long;
Like dry waterless lands, so my soul thirsts for you.
Your love, better than life; on you I gaze,
To see power and glory, on my lips your praise.

Glory, blessing, even in darkness;
All through the night, held by your hand,
Yearning for you.

da Noust

What should we render to Caesar?

Lord, help us to sort out what it means to be good citizens of this state,
but also faithful followers of Jesus, as members of your church.
If our loyalty to the state should conflict with our loyalty to you,
then grant us grace to endure persecution.
Help us to seek peace and justice politically,
but to be faithful to your way of the cross:
to be zealous, but not fanatical;
strong in faith, but not bigoted;
merciful but not sentimental;
to stand up for what is right without arrogant awkwardness.
May we be alive to the issues of the day,
but not carried away by the latest political fashion;
treasure the traditions of the past,
but not be bound by them.
So may we bring glory to our Father in heaven.
King of kings, have mercy upon us and help us to know
what we should render to Caesar
and what we should render to God.

*Mark12:13–17

Ruth Burgess

Palm/Passion Sunday

Opening and closing responses for Palm Sunday

Shout Hosanna

Jesus is coming
SHOUT HOSANNA

He's riding on a donkey
SHOUT HOSANNA

Open the gates
SHOUT HOSANNA

Open the ancient doors
SHOUT HOSANNA

Don't be afraid
SHOUT HOSANNA

Wave the branches
SHOUT HOSANNA

Spread out your coats
SHOUT HOSANNA

Peace in heaven
SHOUT HOSANNA

Glory in highest heaven
SHOUT HOSANNA

(The leader's parts of these responses could be said from different areas of the church by different voices – include children, young people, old people ...)

Lead us into Holy Week

We tell your story
We follow in your footsteps
LEAD US INTO HOLY WEEK

We walk towards the city
We wait in the garden
LEAD US ONTO HOLY GROUND

We journey towards death
We hope for resurrection
LEAD US INTO HOLY JOY

Ruth Burgess

A prayer on the way to Jerusalem

Who may ascend the hill of the Lord?
Who may stand in his holy place?
Those who have clean hands and pure hearts.

O Living God,
age after age the children of dust
make their way to holy places to seek you,
yet you are closer than hands or feet.

In temples and in churches
people make sacrifices and offerings,
but what you seek
is the love and well-being of your children.

Your Word promises
that those whose hands are clean
and whose hearts are pure
can climb the heavenly hill;
but who are we to do that?

On our journey through life
our hearts and our hands
have become stained and dirtied.

If we have stretched out our hands in greed, or lust, or love of money,
LORD, CLEANSE US BY YOUR MERCY.

If our hearts have been sullied by pride or resentment,
LORD, CLEANSE US BY YOUR MERCY.

If we have turned aside from our pilgrimage
to follow the world's ways,
or to seek false gods,
or spirits other than your Holy Spirit,
LORD, CLEANSE US BY YOUR MERCY.

Lord, you forgive the sins of all who turn to you in sincerity;
you cleanse the penitent heart from all uncleanness.
Lord, set our course according to your word
so that we may take up afresh the challenge of the journey to the holy city.

Give us new strength to follow you on your way,
so that even we may ascend the hill of the Lord
and stand in the holy place.
Through Jesus Christ, our Lord. AMEN

Ian Cowie

*Psalm 24

Welcome to the city (but one wee word of advice)

Lord Jesus,
if only you would come to our city like you did to Jerusalem.
We've some great hymns to sing to welcome you!
Our guitars would be out to lead the singing;
we'd wave our scarves and dance.
You would get a real red-carpet welcome –
five-star treatment.

There would be a real religious revival.
It would be wonderful.
If only you would come here
to our country
to rescue us.

But in case you do,
just one wee word of advice –
stick to religion, but be careful.
Don't interfere with politics, or economics, or big business and all that,
and be careful not to make unpopular changes in the way we worship.

Save us from what might happen in the next life, yes,
but leave us to go on our own way,
the way we are used to in this life.

If you get it wrong for our city,
who knows?
We, too, might have to liquidate you.

Ian Cowie

Going up to Jerusalem

Loving God, at this time,
we remember that going up to Jerusalem
cost Jesus his very life.
So we come before you,
conscious of the way religious words
and holy phrases
can slip so easily from our lazy lips
and our hardened hearts.
What do we really know
of your mountainous truth,
your rock-hard integrity,
the depth of your suffering
for love of us all?
Forgive us for the shallowness
of our faith,

and the timidity of our following:
forgive us for the ready excuses
we make for going our own way
and claiming it as yours.

Turn us round again, we pray,
by your Holy Spirit,
active within us and among us.
Show us how to be open again
to your faithfulness
and to your freedom,
that we may live
new lives
and be again bearers
of the seeds of the Kingdom
of Jesus.

John Harvey

Palm Sunday is always happening
A sermon preached in Iona Abbey, Palm Sunday 2004

Oh where are you going
and can I come with you,
and what is your method
for keeping alive:
no pack or possessions,
no clothing or shelter,
no food to sustain you –
how can you survive?

(John L Bell and Graham Maule)

It was a long journey to cover a relatively short distance. Three years it took, beginning with a time of testing; then calling companions, gathering followers, wandering in the Galilee, in a popular ministry which was primarily personal and marked by personal encounters, occasional times of withdrawal in solitude, away from the crowds, sharing intimacy, trying to teach a bunch of quarrelsome misfits (who never really got it) what he was about; and finally the road to Jerusalem, into the glare of national, political, public debate and conflict.

And so Jesus came at last to the city after three years wandering the countryside, ministering to the people who flocked to hear him and to seek healing and hope. He set his face towards Jerusalem, knowing that it held great danger for him. Jerusalem was not a peaceful, prosperous city. It was a city with a history of repeated invasion and attack, in a country occupied by a mighty imperial power. It was a city full of rumours, threat, discontent, where the poorest suffered most, and cried out for a change. It was a city where the pieties of the religious often seemed far removed from the suffering of the people.

Like the people of so many cities throughout history, the people of Jerusalem expected deliverance to come through military force – their own prophets had told the story of conquest often enough.

> *For I am rousing the Chaldeans, that fierce and impetuous nation, who march through the breadth of the earth to seize dwellings not their own. Dread and fearsome are they; their justice and dignity proceed from themselves. Their horses are swifter than leopards, more menacing than wolves at dusk; their horses charge. Their horsemen come from far away; they fly like an eagle swift to devour. They all come for violence, with faces pressing forward; they gather captives like sand.*
>
> *At kings they scoff, and of rulers they make sport. They laugh at every fortress, and heap up earth to take it. Then they sweep by like the wind; they transgress and become guilty; their own might is their god!*
> (Habakkuk 1:6–11, *NRSV*)

But there was always the promise to keep hope alive in testing times, the promise of a Messiah, a deliverer. Many of them looked for a great leader, a warrior hero, to save them. Some of them, as the rumours spread like wildfire through Jerusalem, thought that Jesus might be that leader. Clearly Jesus was aware of that; this was no attempt to slip quietly into the city without anyone noticing. The way he came, the time and manner of his coming, all referred back to the scriptural prophecies, notably that of Zechariah. Jesus came to Jerusalem, and entered it humbly, and riding on a donkey. There is little doubt that the crowds would see Jesus's entry in the light of this prophecy. A donkey was not the customary mount of a warrior or a king. It was the mount of a non-combatant, a civilian, a merchant, perhaps, or even a priest. Zechariah saw the Messiah as the prince of peace, and this was the way Jesus chose to announce himself to Jerusalem.

> *I will remove the war chariots from Israel and take the war horses from Jerusalem; the bows used in battle will be destroyed. Your king will make peace among the nations.*

So said Zechariah.

The prince of peace indeed – but it was a hell of a confrontational way to arrive. This was a mighty challenge: to appear making the most audacious and blasphemous claim, trailing a vagabond army of followers from the north, into a holy city in an occupied territory of the greatest power on earth. It was a challenge to the Pharisees, who did not want anything to upset the Romans, and to threaten the Pharisees' freedom to practise their religion. It was a challenge to Herod, who was already very confused about what was going on. It was a challenge to the military, who didn't want their job of controlling a city, and a country, made any more difficult by yet another popular insurrection. And it was a challenge, or at least a question, to the ordinary people of Jerusalem. *This is who I say I am. Who do you say I am?* This entry to Jerusalem was the most political act of Jesus's life.

And yet, all of them in their different ways missed the point of this public challenge. The Pharisees, scholars and theorists as they were, did not know how to respond to this man who refused to debate or argue with them, hardly spoke to them in fact, but countered their intellectualising by doing things which, infuriatingly, were hard to argue with but which left them feeling foolish and exposed. The military authorities knew how to put down armed uprisings, no one knew better, but had no strategy to deal with someone who offered no violence to anyone and discouraged his followers from violence, while still posing a threat to public order.

And the people? They had crowded the streets of the city to welcome him, and for sure many of them – particularly the poor ones who made up the majority – wanted peace. They wanted an end to occupation, bread in their stomachs, a better life – what people always want. Of course they welcomed him. Oh, but crowds are fickle …Their mood swings, and people follow the crowd. A crowd's a funny thing; it loves a spectacle, it comes out for celebrations and carnivals and joins in with enthusiasm, is good-natured. It comes out equally for death, for funerals and wakes, stands silently or weeps or prays; sometimes it comes out in solidarity, to make a point, to demonstrate a feeling. But a crowd can also turn angry, become threatening, get nasty, do terrible things. What makes the mood swing in a crowd, turns it into a baying mob? What tips the balance between a homecoming and a hanging? What is the energy that races, like lightening, through a crowd?

Was it when they realised that peace was not going to come after a great, bloody, all-conquering battle; that there was going to be no Desert Storm or Operation Freedom – that, for Jesus, peace was not an outcome but a way, and a hard way? Was it when he refused to defend himself with violence? Was it when they realised that if they decided to stand beside Jesus that they would also stand out, become visible, that they would be going against the majority? Was it when he challenged them to make choices that went against all conventional wisdom, that might lead them into danger? Was it when he confronted them with what they knew about themselves but preferred to attribute to others? Was it when they guessed that fullness of life had to go through loss and emptiness first?

Their suspicions were well-founded. Jesus's friends did find themselves on the losing side. They had to give up their quiet lives. They had to give up what security and status they had. They had to give up their previous identity; to let go of their pasts, their family attachments – all of the things that had made them who they were. They had to give up their prejudices and preferences. Some of them had to give up their lives.

Jesus was a lightning conductor for the crowd in Jerusalem. During this last year or so, I have been very aware of many crowds in many cities: in Baghdad and London, in Madrid and Gaza City, in Port-au-Prince and Monrovia, and others you can doubtless name. The moods that rippled through the crowd in Jerusalem have all been visible in these cities, and the challenges. Palm Sunday is always happening, and we are always being confronted by the challenge of that different way of being; the way of peace that does not shrink from conflict but refuses violence, the way that does not theorise but engages with the real needs of suffering people, the way that sees the people who are overlooked and not counted, the way of self-offering. As we walk with Jesus through Holy Week, let us pray for the courage to face these challenges.

O Christ, you entered the city as a poor man,
not in style but simply,
yet still you caused uproar, and questions everywhere;
you drew the expectations of a hungry crowd,
and brought buried conflicts to the light.
May we, who are sometimes swayed by the crowd's approval,
and who often avoid conflict
for fear of its cost to us,
hold fast to the gospel of peace and justice
and follow faithfully in your way of compassion and solidarity
with those who are poor and excluded,
wherever it may lead us.
Amen

Kathy Galloway

A home liturgy for Holy Week

This liturgy takes place each day during Holy Week, at the family table, during a meal. The youngest person able to asks the questions.

Items needed: Six candles (one of them red) in holders; a palm cross; a copy of the Lord's prayer; a bottle of perfume; a purse filled with money; a bowl of perfumed water and a hand towel; a wooden cross; the makings of an Easter garden; a special Easter candle.

Palm Sunday

Place six candles on the family table and arrange them in the shape of a circle. Light the six candles. Place a palm cross (brought from church?) on the table, in the centre of the circle.

Reading: Mark 11:1–11

Question: 'Why do we have six candles and this palm cross on the table today?'

Answer: 'Because this week is Holy Week. In six days it's Good Friday, and Easter is coming. Today we remember how all the people welcomed Jesus into Jerusalem by waving palm branches.'

Holy Monday

Light five candles (of the circle of six). Place a copy of the Lord's prayer on the table, in the centre of the circle of candles.

Reading: Mark 11:15–19

Question: 'Why do we have five candles and the Lord's Prayer on the table today?'

Answer: 'Because this week is Holy Week. In five days it's Good Friday, and Easter is coming. Today we remember that Jesus threw the money-changers out of the temple. "My house shall be called a place of prayer," he told them. His special prayer is for us all.'

Say or read the Lord's prayer together.

Holy Tuesday

Light four candles. Place a bottle of perfume on the table, in the centre of the circle of candles.

Reading: Mark 14:3–9

Question: 'Why do we have four candles and some perfume on the table today?'

Answer: 'Because this week is Holy Week. In four days it's Good Friday, and Easter is coming. Today we remember the woman from Bethany who anointed Jesus's head, who recognised that he was the King of kings and would soon die.'

Holy Wednesday

Light three candles. Place a purse filled with money in the centre of the circle of candles.

Reading: Mark 14:10–11

Question: 'Why do we have three candles and this purse full of money on the table today?'

Answer: 'Because this week is Holy Week. In three days it's Good Friday, and Easter is coming. Today we remember that Jesus was betrayed for money, and that Jesus wants us to give what we can to help those in the world who are poor.'

(The family could discuss right and wrong ways of using money, in the light of today's and yesterday's readings.)

Maundy Thursday

Light two candles. Have a bowl of warm water and a towel on the table between them. The family wash each others' hands before the meal. The meal could include elements of a Passover meal (unleavened bread, wine…).

Reading: Mark 14:22–26; John 13:2–5,12–15

Question: 'Why do we have two candles and this towel and water on the table today?'

Answer: 'Because this is Holy Week. One candle is for Good Friday, and one is for today, Maundy Thursday. Today we remember the last Passover meal that Jesus celebrated with his disciples. Our communion service derives from this meal.'

Good Friday

The one red candle is lit – and then blown out. A wooden cross is placed on the table. The palm cross is blu-tacked to the front door until the Sunday after Easter or until Pentecost.

Question: 'Why did we blow out the candle today?'

Answer: 'Today is Good Friday. This is day that we remember that Jesus died and went home to God.'

Reading: Mark 15:21–39

Everyone is quiet for a few minutes.

Holy Saturday

Reading: Mark 15:42–47

The family together make an Easter garden on a tray or plate. An Easter garden includes a model of a cave, with a stone that can be rolled away on Easter Day. (The cave represents the tomb where Jesus was buried.) Spring flowers are traditionally included in the garden. Let your creativity play.

Easter Day

Light seven candles (the circle of six and the special Easter candle in the centre of the circle). Roll away the stone from the cave/tomb and light a candle beside it. Have on the table: spring flowers beside the circle of candles, Easter eggs, and whatever else you like to make the table festive.

Reading: John 20:11–18

Question: 'Why do we have Easter eggs and all these flowers and candles today?'

Answer: 'Because today is Easter Day, the last day of Holy Week. Today we remember that Jesus rose from the dead and showed us the new life God offers all of us, not just after we die but through the difficult bits of living now.'

If sufficiently extrovert, people cheer or shout Alleluia!

Chris Polhill

Palm Sunday evening

This time
there will be no flight into Egypt.
This donkey has too much to carry,
too far.

The shadows wait for me:
around the table at Passover,
among those in high places,
in the condemned cell,
on the hill outside.

Fear haunts my waking moments
and I cannot sleep.
Why has God forsaken me?

The crowd today is with me,
but not for long.
They are the powerless ones
(the ones who matter).
The ones who count
are counting.

Time is running out.
This time
there will be no flight into Egypt.

Josie Smith

Monday, Tuesday and Wednesday of Holy Week

Readings and responses:

Monday – Is 42:1–7; Ps 26 or 36:5–11; Jn:12:1–11

Tuesday – Is 49:1–6; Ps 70 or 71:1–14; Jn:13:21–33, 36–38 or 12:20–36

Wednesday – Is 50:4–9; Ps 68 or 70; Mt:26:14–25 or John 13:21–32

A bruised reed

When we bruise
like a reed in the wind
JESUS TEND US

When we wane
like a flickering lamp
JESUS SHIELD US

When we lose courage
and walk without hope
JESUS CHEER US

God's constant love

God, your constant love reaches the heavens
YOUR FAITHFULNESS EXTENDS TO THE SKIES

Your righteousness is towering like the mountains
YOUR JUSTICE IS LIKE THE DEPTHS OF THE SEA

How precious is your constant love
WE FIND PROTECTION UNDER THE SHADOW OF YOUR WINGS

You are the source of all life
AND BECAUSE OF YOUR LIGHT, WE SEE THE LIGHT.

Psalm 36:5–9 (Good News Bible)

Generous God

Generous God
Bringer of justice
YOU ARE THE SOURCE OF OUR TRUTH

Gathering God
Lover of courage
YOU ARE THE SOURCE OF OUR STRENGTH

Glorious God
Light of the nations
YOU ARE THE SOURCE OF OUR JOY

God of Jew and Gentile

God of Jew and Gentile
Walking the streets of Jerusalem
YOUR LIFE IS AT RISK

God of Jew and Gentile
Sharing your food and your stories
YOUR LIFE IS AT RISK

God of Jew and Gentile
Waiting for someone to betray you
YOUR LIFE IS AT RISK

Ruth Burgess

A story from Iona

On Iona, in the early days of the Iona Community, it was decided to commission a well-known glassmaker to make six glass communion cups for use in the Abbey. The craftsman was asked to engrave a suitable biblical text on each of the cups: 'This the blood of the new covenant', 'This do in remembrance of me', and so on. Now this craftsman, as it happened, was not a churchman, although he was sympathetic to 'Christianity'. And when he received the commission he made one request: Could he choose one of the texts to engrave on the cups? His request was granted.

And when the cups were delivered, the folk on Iona were intrigued to discover that the text he had chosen was from the arrest of Jesus in the garden of Gethsemane, when Judas betrays Jesus with a kiss. And the text that he had engraved on the cup was Jesus's question to Judas: 'Friend, wherefore art thou come?'

John Harvey

One man and his boss

(This piece is written for two voices. Speaker 1 is seen and heard counting out coins.)

One
This is a story about a man and his boss.
Two
Our man joined the firm with eleven others.
Three
They were all equal partners under one boss.
Four
The boss was a good man – they all trusted him.
Five
Our man was respected by the firm; they put him in charge
of finances.
Six
He kept a tight ship – he hated waste.
Seven
Occasionally, he was tempted to dip into the money for his own use – but that was one of the perks of the job.
Eight
The firm travelled a lot, moving around the country.

Nine

The boss took risks – he offended the establishment; he didn't always mix with the right kind of people – and where the boss went, the firm went too.

Ten

Our man didn't always approve of the company the firm kept, but he kept his thoughts to himself.

Eleven

Sometimes the group split up and operated in pairs – the boss trusted them to do this.

Twelve

They discovered that they could do most of the things the boss could do; they were excited and pleased.

Thirteen

The firm stayed together for three years – they were good together.

Fourteen

The partners did not always agree about what the boss had asked them to do – there were sometimes arguments.

Fifteen

The boss settled arguments quickly – they knew that he was fair; he tried not to have favourites.

Sixteen

Our man had clear ideas about what he wanted from the firm and where he wanted the boss to take them.

Seventeen

As the days went on the boss appeared, to our man, to be getting fanatical about challenging the establishment.

Eighteen

Our man could see where things were heading and he wanted out.

Nineteen

Our man had choices: he could try to persuade the boss to change direction, but that seemed unlikely, or he could go to the establishment and offer them a way to bring the firm down.

Twenty

Our man sensed that the boss knew what he was up to – if the other partners discovered what he was up to he was in trouble. But if the boss was choosing not to tell them, maybe he secretly approved of what our man was contemplating and wanted him to do it, or maybe he didn't – it was a chance our man would have to take.

Twenty-one

What finally led our man to take action was the night the boss turned on him for criticising a woman – all that talk of 'the poor' and 'death and burial'; that might be the way the boss intended to go but our man had no intention of following him.

Twenty-two

Our man went to the establishment and spilled the beans. They wanted to interview the boss in person and he agreed to lead their militia to him. They paid our man well – in silver.

Twenty-three

One night, while the firm, still blissfully unaware, enjoyed their annual dinner, the boss hinted strongly that he knew what our man was doing. After an exchange of words with the boss, our man left the meal early to do the deed.

Twenty-four

He led the militia to a secret garden where he knew that the boss and his partners would be – he pointed to the boss and then kissed him. The soldiers acted on his signal and the boss was arrested and taken away.

Twenty-five

Our man breathed a sigh of relief – he was now on the side of the establishment; even if the partners tried to get back at him (they had little chance) their reputations, with the boss arrested, would be in tatters.

Twenty-six

Later he heard the news: the establishment had sentenced the boss to death. He'd not meant that; he thought they'd just … well, he wasn't sure what he'd thought – but he hadn't wanted anyone to be killed. And he certainly didn't want to be blamed or held responsible for the boss's death.

Twenty-seven

He went back to the establishment; he tried to tell them that the boss was really a good man, foolish maybe, deserving punishment perhaps, but not death. He tried to give them back the money they'd paid him, said he'd made a mistake, and they laughed at him and told him to go away; and he did, throwing the money down on the floor as he ran out.

Twenty-eight

Our man could not cope. He hung himself.

He died by his own hand and his boss died at the hands of strangers.

Twenty-nine

The firm broke up. The partners went into hiding

Thirty – yes, that's it, thirty pieces of silver:

The money they paid our man Judas to betray his boss, Jesus.

They're going to use it, somewhat fittingly, to buy a burial ground.

Ruth Burgess

Terrible love

How wonderful and how terrible is your love, O God.

The love which weeps with longing for your children
while they plan to crucify you.

The love which longs to enfold them as a hen enfolds her chicks,
but which is spread-eagled on a cross to die in agony.

The love which allows us to go the way we have wrongly chosen,
but which follows us into our Godforsaken-ness.

How wonderful and how terrible is your love, O God;
before that mystery we bow.

May we know that enfolding love now, as we turn from our folly
to the love which created us,
the love which comes to save us,
the love which will never let us go.

In the silence now, may your enfolding love reach each one of us.

(*Silence*)

For the assurance of your love given to us afresh,
thanks be to God, through Jesus Christ, our Lord. AMEN

With your love to enfold us and your peace to uphold us,
WE GO ON OUR WAY.
With your word to guide us and your heavenly host to guard us,
WE GO ON OUR WAY.
With the fellowship of the Holy Spirit between us, and your blessing on our homes,
WE GO ON OUR WAY.

Glory be to God the Father whose love is over us.
Glory be to Jesus whose love shares our human lives.
Glory be to the Holy Spirit alive and powerful as love within us.
To the One God, eternally love, be glory and praise for ever. **Amen**

Ian Cowie

Matthew 23:37,39

Scented love

♩ = 126
Flute introduction

Were I, your Lord and Mas - ter, to kneel be - fore your bo - dy, cra - dl - ing your weak - ness, I would bathe your fears. My heal - ing touch re - mem - bers love, scent - ed love from Ma - ry, bro - ken jar of oint - ment, feet im - mersed in tears.

Were

da Noust

Bird's-Eye View
John 2:13–22

A: Croo

B: Croo

A: Croo

B: Coo – that was a near thing!

A: You got away, too!

B: Who wouldn't take such a chance of freedom? I flew right up to the roof.

A: I like the view.

B: The bird's-eye view. Me too.

A: Too

B: Too

A: Too

B: They are milling round down there.

A: They don't know what's hit them – what a kerfuffle!

B: Jesus certainly ruffled a few feathers …

A: And saved our necks into the bargain. Why did he do it?

B: Animal liberation? There were cattle and sheep, too.

A: But the money changers – what did he have against them?

B: Didn't you hear what he said to the dealer in pigeons?

A: Don't mention those villains!

B: He said, 'You must not turn my Father's house into a market.'

A: Quite right too!

B: Too

A: Too

B: Too

A: His Father's house?

B: He meant the temple here.

A: It's home for quite a few – the sparrows and swallows, who build their nests up in the roof; the human beings, who are here singing praise to God, day by day.

B: But the buyers and sellers, they made themselves quite at home: they set their tables, paid for pitches, built pens for the sheep and cattle …

A: Brought us along, in our cages, to wait for a family to come: 'Two pigeons please, to offer on the altar as we bring our baby son to the temple.'

B: Lovely child – pity about the pigeons!

A: It probably happened when Jesus was born: being welcomed into his Father's house with a child-size sacrifice, a few white feathers fluttering down …

B: Well, we've survived to fly another day!

A: Phew

B: Phew

A: Phew

B: Phew

A: Why did he save our lives?

B: Why did he drive out the dealers?

A: Why did he scatter the money?

B: Why did he say, 'You must not turn my Father's house into a market?'

A: Because the temple is special?

B: It's big.

A: It's old.

B: It took years to build.

A: It's where people worship …

B: When they're not being distracted by 'baas' and 'moos' and money clinking and people driving hard bargains.

A: Between me and you …

B: You

A: You

B: You

A: Yes – look at us – we are special. People sometimes see doves as a sign of God's presence. It didn't stop them sacrificing us!

B: People call this place 'God's house' – but it didn't stop them turning it into a market place.

A: They can see – if they have eyes – that Jesus, with his whip and his anger, or with his healing hands and caring or the words he speaks …

B: Look how they are listening now –

A: They can see that Jesus is someone special … but that won't stop them killing him.

B: Don't say that! Just like the lambs and us doves, sacrificed for their sins. People – they spoil everything!

A: But he'll be back. He's God's home – a temple they can't destroy.

B: He's God's love that they can't kill.

A: He's a dove that they can't cage …

B: One day he'll fly free in the world

A: Like me and you …

B: Croo

A: Croo

B: Croo

Jan Sutch Pickard

I owed him one

I knew what
I had to do
but I didn't want to do it.

I owed him one –
he had brought my brother
back from the grave
and it had cost him.

It wasn't the first time he'd done it,
there had been others too:
a daughter of a synagogue official,
a son of a widow.
He knew what he was doing.

And he knew now
that he was going to die
very soon.
His disciples refused to
believe him.

I didn't want to lose him
but I didn't want
to hold him back.
I knew
that he must walk
his own road.

I wanted to help him,
but how do you help
someone you love
get ready for death?
It's a hard question
without an easy answer.

All that I could think of
was the perfume that I had used
to anoint my brother's body for burial.
What I had done for Lazarus' dead body
I could do for Jesus' live one.

And I did.

And when I heard him
telling people
that I had helped him
to prepare for his death and burial,
I knew that he had understood.

I love you Jesus.

Ruth Burgess

*John 12:1–8

Havens of welcome

Lord Jesus,
we give thanks that, in the midst of so much ill-feeling and misunderstanding,
there were people at Bethany who welcomed you.

And we give thanks that, down the ages, there have been those who, in their
homes, have offered havens of welcome and understanding in the midst of strife.

We give thanks for those who have opened their homes to us
when we needed somewhere to find refuge.

May our hearts and homes be like that home in Bethany:
places of understanding for the misunderstood,
places of peace for the hunted,
places of healing for the suffering.

Lord Jesus,
make yourself at home in us.
We know that you will take us as you find us –
so just come in.

Ian Cowie

The Judas and Mary in us
(An evening meditation)

In the quietness of this evening time,
we ponder the strange interweaving of the love of God
with both human sin and human goodness.
Sin and goodness write a story in each of our lives.
In each of us, and in each congregation, both Mary and Judas are to be found.
But we know, too, that the love of God in Christ redeems it all.

Therefore, in quietness, let us confront the Judas in us who could spoil everything,
and allow the Mary in each of us to find some beautiful thing to do for God.

We will have three minutes of silence (or music).

O God ... what can we do for you?

Silence or music

What we have purposed in our hearts, enable us to carry through.

Silence the sensible disciple in us who would think it a waste.
Silence the Judas in us who would begrudge the money and the effort.

Nothing is too good for you, Lord.
Nobody is too bad for you to love.

May we individually, and our church as a whole,
be known for the extravagant love which makes us fools for Christ's sake.

A hymn of dedication

In your peace we go to our homes;
in your love we will take our rest;
in your light may we rise tomorrow to follow you afresh. Amen

Ian Cowie

*John 12:1–7

The way of the cross

Jesus,
as we start once again
to follow you
on the way of the cross,
we are apprehensive.
For we are not sure
of ourselves.
On our journey
we have often been afraid,
often sought the safe options,
often fudged the sharp solution.
On our journey
we have often tried to hide
our real selves
from others,
from ourselves
and from you.
We, who dare to say
we are following you,
know how faltering are our footsteps,
how delicate our discipleships,
how feeble our faith.

Yet still you call us
by name
and invite us into your company
and onto your road.
So give us the courage
and the commitment we need:
help us to look out for one another on the road;
show us how we may share the duty
and the joy
of discipleship,

knowing that, in the end,
it is you who have blazed the trail,
you who accompany us all the way,
you who will meet us on the road,
and say our name. Amen

John Harvey

A job's a job

I do some daft things for money
but I was broke.
I'd just moved into the city
and my mate, David's dad – Mr Cohen –
was looking for someone
to run a message for him.

So – in for an assarion, in for a denarius –
I went over to see him.

It's only a little job Daniel, he said.
Bit of waiting around,
nothing too arduous –
but you'll have to agree to do it
before I can give you the details.
It's all a bit hush hush, you see.

So I agreed,
and he told me all about it.
It was on for tomorrow.
All I had to do was to hang around in the city centre
until a bloke spotted me
and nodded in my direction …

And then I had to walk back slowly to Mr Cohen's house
and let this bloke follow me.

You see, Daniel, said Mr Cohen,
I can't let David do it.
It would be too obvious.
Everyone round here knows that he's got lots of sisters,
but you're new round here.
You'll look strange,
but nobody will know why you're doing such a job.

Strange – I'd look strange all right.
The way that they'd worked out that this bloke would spot me
was that I'd be carrying a jar of water!
The women would have a field day.
A man carrying water?
I could hear them now:
'What's the matter son? Is your girlfriend allergic to the wet stuff?'
'Away my bonnie lad, let me carry your jar for you and I'll show you how
my muscles work!'
And those would be the polite ones!

Well, I can't say I'm looking forward to tomorrow,
but a job's a job;
and if I wear something that I can get rid of afterwards,
maybe no one will ever know
that it was me.

Ruth Burgess

Mark 14:13–16

Maundy Thursday

A Passover meal for thirteen

How come it's always me that gets to lay the table and never the boys?
A Passover meal for thirteen, mum says,
in our upstairs room;
ten courses,
best dishes,
two jars of wine,
and they might need a waitress.
Job for you, Naomi, mum says.
Maybe a bit of pocket money in it –
you'd like that, wouldn't you?

Me – I'd rather be out playing with my friends,
but what choice do I get?

So here I am
setting the table for thirteen.
Best cloths, Passover dishes, best cutlery – the works!
I wheedled it out of mum that the meal
is for Jesus and his friends,
but I've got to keep it secret.
They don't want their enemies
to burst in and disturb them.
Mum's a bit scared about there being trouble.
Jesus has been known to liven up a few parties –
the water and the wine mystery
and the perfume in the parlour scandal
to name but two.
But I'm sure mum needn't worry.
Jesus is our friend,
I'm sure he wouldn't cause trouble for her.

But all the same
I'm going to keep my eyes and ears open tonight –
I might have a few stories later
to share with my friends.

Ruth Burgess

*Mark 14:15

Prayer before going to church on Maundy Thursday

I will walk in the wind
to meet you Jesus
to let you wash my feet.
I don't want to.
I would rather stay here in the warm,
away from your towels and water
and offers of forgiveness,
for I know what you mean,
what you ask,
what you give.

But I will come,
for I cannot stay here alone,
and I cannot run elsewhere,
for I know that you are waiting,
welcoming.
And I know that only you
can heal me and hold me.

So I will come
with empty hands to your supper,
empty hands and dirty feet.
I will come as your guest
and with water, bread and wine
you will make me whole
and set me free to serve you.

Ruth Burgess

The cloud of witnesses
(A beginning and an ending for a Maundy Thursday liturgy)

Beginning

They gathered in an upper room to share a meal.

And the names of the apostles were these:
Simon, called Peter,
his brother Andrew;
James
and his brother John – the sons of Zebedee;
Philip
and Bartholomew;
Thomas
and Matthew the tax collector;
James the son of Alphaeus,
Thaddaeus;
Simon the patriot,
and Judas Iscariot. (Matthew 10:2–4)

(As each name is read a candle is lit or, instead, 12 people take a name and a candle each, speaking a name and lighting a candle in turn round a table. You might want to include the women who travelled with Jesus and shared his ministry. Luke 8:1–3)

Seeing that we are surrounded with such a great cloud of witnesses to faith –
those who ran their races before us and have entered into their rests –
we join with them now to praise your name.

For the first apostles,
and for all those who have kept the light of the gospel burning down the centuries,
we give thanks.

For those who went before us and passed the light on to us,
especially those whom we remember now …
we give thanks.

Come, Lord Jesus,
take your rightful place as host at this, your table.

(A large central candle is lit.)

Ending

After the meal Jesus and his disciples sang a hymn and they went out to the Mount of Olives. Jesus said to them, 'All of you will run away and leave me, for the scripture says, "God will kill the shepherd and the sheep of the flock will be scattered".' (Matthew 26:31)

Jesus went with them to a place called Gethsemane.

He was arrested and they all forsook him and fled.

(In silence, the candles are extinguished, one at a time in reverse order, beginning with Judas Iscariot's candle and ending with Simon Peter's. The large candle symbolising Jesus is carried out of the room, still alight.)

Ian Cowie

A story from Birmingham

He was only a little lad was Leonard –
well, he was five, nearly,
and he had a big brother, Dean, who was eight,
and they both lived round the corner from me.

It was Maundy Thursday,
and a few of us were celebrating it in a friend's flat;
and we'd got to the bit in the story
where Jesus washed the disciples' feet.

We sometimes acted things out.
We said it was to help the kids
understand the story,
but most of the grown-ups liked to do it too.

The washing-up bowl
was full of warm water
and soapy bubbles,
and Leonard had been invited
to wash his brother's feet.

It was a task
undertaken with utter seriousness
and with laughter,
and infectious joy.
Wash his feet?
Soap him up to the knees more like!
Cup and splash the water over his ankles,
and tickle him under his toes.
Bathtime had nothing on this!

Leonard had bubbles dancing in all directions
and lather running back
down his arms
into his turned-up sleeves.
And he followed up the washing
with a thorough
drying,
with fluffy towels.
All the way down
from the knees to the toes.

Later came shared bread rolls,
previously kneaded by small fists
and baked in the oven,
and a common mug of juice
that had been trampled and squeezed
from purple grapes.

When I sit sometimes
in other gatherings –
where it is hard to
find volunteers
on a Maundy Thursday
to have one foot
gently washed and dried
by a kneeling priest –
I recall,
with yearning,

the story of Dean and Leonard,
and the washing and drying
of feet
and knees
and toes.

Ruth Burgess

A prayer before the washing of feet

God of dirty hands and tired feet,
taking people as they come,
kneeling and healing,
touching where others turn away,
forgive us when we want to be too clean.
Forgive us when we despise life
for the messy business it is.

If we are too proud
to own up to our brokenness,
if we keep hidden
what needs refreshment,
how can you care for us?

Silence

You can care – and this is how:
when we are ready to move
from distance to involvement,
from intent to touch,
then you will wash the feet
that tire on rocky roads;
you will care and heal
beyond our expectation.

Thanks be to God. AMEN

David Coleman

If I, your Lord and Master

da Noust

It makes me weep rivers that bit

Ah couldnie dae whit ye've done, Jesus.
Ah'm scared o' dark an' powerful forces.
Ah prefer to run an' hide,
maybe kick their bums when they're no lookin'.
But in the main … Ah'm feart.

You spread joy among despondency.
Noo here, Ah've hid wee successes maself.

You came to crush the oppressors.
Aye, Ah'm right behind ye there.
But Ah should explain …
sometimes Ah cannie stand ma ground.

You rallied against cant an' hypocracy.
So dae Ah.
Then Ah start usin' them masel'
(cause it's easier an softer) an cringe.

You healed the sick wi' yer love.
Ah'd like tae dae that
but lack the currency.

But see you!
in the garden of Gestemenie.
Could ye no hav ran
or at least hooked Judas?

Jist standin' there, lettin' them do ye in.
It makes me weep rivers that bit.

Stuart Barrie

Here's a man

Here's a man,
born to a mother who broke the rules and said 'yes',
parented by a man who was not his father,
knowing his ancient lineage
yet calling people to be born again into a new community.

Here's a man,
tramping the dusty roads of his country,
drawing inspiration from the land,
loving its fruitfulness,
sailing its waters,
stilling its storms.

Here's a man,
throwing up a steady job to follow his calling,
keeping bad company, often sleeping rough,
touching people who were considered untouchable,
raising up those who were overlooked.

Here's a man,
refusing to be less than free,
refusing to be less than utterly committed,
refusing to bow down and serve the empires of the world;
in tenderness, justice and joy,
in forgiving and healing,
he lived the promise of a new relationship with God.

He was called by many names.
He called himself 'the Son of Man'.

Kathy Galloway

Good Friday

Stations of the Cross

First Station: Jesus is condemned to death

Optional response to precede each Station of the Cross:

We adore you, O Christ, and we bless you
BECAUSE, BY YOUR HOLY CROSS, YOU HAVE REDEEMED THE WORLD.

Bible Reading – Mark 15:1–5,11–15

Jesus was taken in chains to Pilate. The chief priests were accusing Jesus of many things, so Pilate questioned him. 'Aren't you going to answer?' he said. 'Listen to all their accusations.' Jesus refused to say a word and Pilate was amazed.

Pilate spoke to the crowd. 'What do you want me to do with this one you call King of the Jews?' They shouted back, 'Crucify him!'

'But what crime has he committed?' Pilate asked.

They shouted all the louder, 'Crucify him!'

Pilate wanted to please the crowd, so he set Barabbas free for them. Then he had Jesus whipped and handed him over to be crucified.

Meditation

Pilate asked what crime Jesus had committed.
It was a good question.
Jesus had annoyed the religious leaders, of that there was no doubt.
He had been critical of social and religious structures.
He had healed the villagers;
he had told stories to the crowds;
he was probably a threat to public law and order;
but was that enough to condemn him, to end his life?
But he would not defend himself –
the storyteller was silent now
and the crowd was noisy,
and Pilate handed him over to be crucified.

Prayer

For those on trial this week and for those appointed to judge them:
God in your mercy,
HEAR OUR PRAYER.

Optional chant between each station: 'Jesus, remember me when you come into your Kingdom' (Taizé) or 'Behold the Lamb of God' (John L Bell and Graham Maule).

Second Station: Jesus takes up his cross

Bible reading – Mark 15:16–20

The soldiers took Jesus inside, to the courtyard of the governor's palace and called together the rest of the company. They put a purple robe on Jesus, made a crown out of thorn branches, and put it on his head. Then they began to salute him:

'Long live the King of the Jews.' They beat him over the head with a stick, spat on him, fell on their knees and bowed to him.

When they had finished mocking him, they took off the purple robe and put his own clothes back on him. Then they led him out to crucify him.

Meditation

Soldiers
taking the chance for a bit of fun.
They had a heavy day ahead.
Soon they would have to put on their public face –
disciplined, controlled, efficient.
But for now a bit of a lark with the lads
with no risk of recrimination.
Dead men tell no stories,
and Jesus was going to his death.

Prayer

For those appointed to keep public order,
and for those tempted to abuse their power:
God in your mercy,
HEAR OUR PRAYER.

Third Station: Jesus falls the first time

Bible reading – Isaiah 53:1

Who would have believed what we now tell?
Who could have seen God's hand in this?

Meditation

Jesus was exhausted.
He was in pain.
He was going to his death.

The cross was heavy and he fell.
He was flesh and blood like us,
he was struggling.

Prayer

For those who are tired or in pain:
God in your mercy,
HEAR OUR PRAYER.

Fourth Station: Jesus meets his mother

Bible reading – Luke 2:22,25,34,35

The time came for Joseph and Mary to perform the ceremony of purification as the Law of Moses commanded. So they took the child Jesus to Jerusalem to present him to the Lord.

At that time there was a man named Simeon living in Jerusalem. Simeon blessed them and said to Mary, 'This child is chosen by God for the destruction and salvation of many in Israel. He will be a sign from God which many people will speak against and so reveal their secret thoughts. And sorrow, like a sharp sword, will break your own heart.'

Meditation

She was going to be there at his end –
she who had been there with God at his beginning.
She was his mother.
She had fed him and cradled him
and watched over his growing.
Whatever he had said and done,
he was still her son
and she would not desert him now.
Whatever pain of his she could embrace she would.
And in the meeting of their eyes
there was love,
suffering and shining.

Prayer

For parents whose children are in pain or in trouble:
God in your mercy,
HEAR OUR PRAYER.

Fifth Station: Simon helps Jesus to carry his cross

Bible reading – Mark 15:21

On their way through Jerusalem they met a man named Simon, who was coming into the city from the country, and the soldiers forced him to carry Jesus' cross.

Meditation

Simon from Cyrene,
father of Alexander and Rufus,
what a tale you had to tell your children!
You helped Jesus,
you gave him your strength on the streets of Jerusalem.
Willing or unwilling,
you, Simon, have become part of his story,
and he part of yours,
for you helped him
when he needed you.
What would we give to be Simon?

Prayer

For a willingness to serve you, in friends and in strangers,
God in your mercy,
HEAR OUR PRAYER.

Sixth Station: Veronica wipes the face of Jesus

Bible reading – Matthew 25:35–36,40

I was hungry and you fed me,
thirsty, and you gave me a drink.
I was a stranger and you received me in your homes,
naked and you clothed me;
I was sick and you took care of me,
in prison and you visited me.
Whenever you did this – you did it for me.

Meditation

Wiping faces, dirty faces;
faces full of sweat and tears,

faces covered in chocolate and in jam.
Wiping faces is something we try to do gently and lovingly,
something that soothes and cleanses,
something that brings healing.
Wiping faces is something we do for those who are young, or old,
or in pain, or in trouble,
wanting them to know that they are cherished and loved.
And when we wipe the faces of God's little ones,
we are wiping the face of God.

Prayer

For those whose faces we wipe
and for those who wipe away our tears:
God in your mercy,
HEAR OUR PRAYER.

Seventh Station: Jesus falls the second time

Bible reading – Isaiah 53:7

Ill-treated and afflicted,
he never said a word.
Like a lamb led to the slaughter house,
like a sheep dumb before its shearers,
he never opened his mouth.

Meditation

I am finding it hard to watch you, Jesus,
to see you struggling,
to see you on the ground.
Into your silence I want to shout:
'Why do they keep on hurting you?
What have you done wrong?'

Prayer

For those who today will struggle and fall:
God in your mercy,
HEAR OUR PRAYER.

Eighth Station: Jesus meets the women of Jerusalem

Bible reading – Luke 23:27,28

A large crowd of people followed Jesus; among them were some women who were weeping and wailing for him. Jesus turned to them and said, 'Women of Jerusalem, don't cry for me, but for yourselves and for your children.'

Meditation

Weep for the mothers and children of Jerusalem,
for Israeli and Palestinian,
for Jew and Moslem and Christian,
for the strangers in their midst.
Pray for the peace of Jerusalem.
Pray that her people may live together in justice.
Pray that all people may live together in peace.

Prayer

For those who live in places of conflict and danger;
for peacemakers and peacekeepers in every land:
God in your mercy,
HEAR OUR PRAYER.

Ninth Station: Jesus falls the third time

Bible reading – Isaiah 53:4–5

He endured the suffering that should have been ours,
the pain we should have borne.
All the while we thought that his suffering was punishment sent by God;
but because of our sins he was wounded,
beaten because of the evil we did.
We are healed by the punishment he suffered,
made whole by the blows he received.

Meditation

I am not sure if I can watch this much longer.
In his pain I see my pain,
in his falling I feel myself falling,

in his cross ... in his cross
I am included.
He carried it for me –
for me, and my enemies, and my friends.

Prayer

For those whom I love,
for those whom I struggle to love,
for those who find me difficult:
God in your mercy,
HEAR OUR PRAYER.

Tenth Station: Jesus is stripped of his clothes

Bible reading – Mark 15:22–24

They took Jesus to a place called Golgotha, which means the place of the skull. They tried to give him wine mixed with a drug called myrrh, but Jesus would not drink it. Then they crucified him and divided his clothing among themselves, throwing dice to see who would get each piece of clothing.

Meditation

Stripped now –
of clothing
of disciples
of friends.
Alone,
naked and vulnerable,
with nothing to protect you from the pain to come.

Prayer

For those deserted by friends,
for those who are alone and vulnerable:
God in your mercy,
HEAR OUR PRAYER.

Eleventh Station: Jesus is nailed to the cross

Bible reading – Luke 23:35,49

It was nine o'clock in the morning when they crucified him; the people stayed there watching him, the leaders jeered at him and the soldiers mocked him. Some women, his friends from Galilee, looked on at a distance.

Meditation

We look on from a distance:
a distance of time and space and culture,
a distance of *a Sunday afternoon in England** in Lent.
And for us it hurts to watch Jesus dying,
even at a distance.
It hurts to know that we are being rescued.
It hurts to know how much we are valued and loved.

*(*Change as appropriate)*

Prayer

For the depth of your love for us, we thank you.
God in your mercy,
HEAR OUR PRAYER.

Twelfth Station: Jesus dies on the cross

Bible reading – Luke 23:44–46

It was about twelve o'clock when the sun stopped shining and darkness covered the whole country until three o'clock. And the curtain hanging in the Temple was torn in two. Jesus cried out in a loud voice, 'Father in your hands I place my spirit.' He said this and died.

Meditation

In your hands he placed himself:
all that he was,
all that he had ever been,
all his beauty,
all his obedience,
all his loving.

In God's hands he placed himself.
He was returning to his father,
he was going home.

Prayer

For all who have died today,
for all who love them and will miss them:
God in your mercy,
HEAR OUR PRAYER.

Thirteenth Station: Jesus is taken down from the cross

Bible reading – Mark 15:42–46

And when evening came, Joseph of Arimathea, a respected member of the council, went to Pilate and asked for the body of Jesus. Joseph took the body down and wrapped it in a linen sheet.

Meditation

Pietà.
Jesus is dead and lies in the arms of his mother.
Death is hard and final
and yet, whatever happens on this earth,
children never die to their mothers.
In the memory of those who loved them, loved ones remain.
And for us, and for all God's people,
our hope is safe in God.
From swaddling bands to grave clothes,
all the days of our living and dying,
we are cradled and wrapped in love.

Prayer

For our families and friends who have died,
for ourselves as we carry their stories:
God in your mercy,
HEAR OUR PRAYER.

Fourteenth Station: Jesus is laid in the tomb

Bible reading – Mark 15:46–47

Joseph placed the body in a tomb which had been dug out of solid rock. Then he rolled a large stone across the entrance. Mary Magdalene and Mary the mother of Joseph were watching and saw where the body of Jesus was placed.

Meditation

The door is shut now,
and the world sighs and waits.
And we wait in night's darkness,
longing for the morning,
longing for the light.

Prayer

For all who are waiting.
For all who are longing for light:
God in your mercy,
HEAR OUR PRAYER.

Fifteenth Station: The resurrection

Bible reading – Mark 16:1–7

After the Sabbath was over, Mary Magdalene, Mary the mother of James, and Salome brought spices to anoint the body of Jesus. Very early on Sunday morning, at sunrise, they went to the tomb. On the way they said to one another, 'Who will roll away the stone for us from the entrance to the tomb?' It was a very large stone. Then they looked up and saw that the stone had already been rolled back. So they entered the tomb, where they saw a young man sitting on the right wearing a white robe, and they were alarmed. 'Don't be alarmed,' he said. 'I know you are looking for Jesus of Nazareth who was crucified. He is not here. He has been raised. Look! Here is the place where they put him. Now go and give this message to his disciples, including Peter: He is going to Galilee ahead of you. There you will see Him, just as He told you.'

Meditation

We go on our way
and Jesus goes ahead of us.
We do not need to be afraid

for Jesus is risen.
God is love –
and love is more powerful
than fear or death or evil,
and we are greatly loved.
And we are grateful.
Thanks be to God for redeeming the world in love. AMEN

Ruth Burgess

Jesus carries the cross

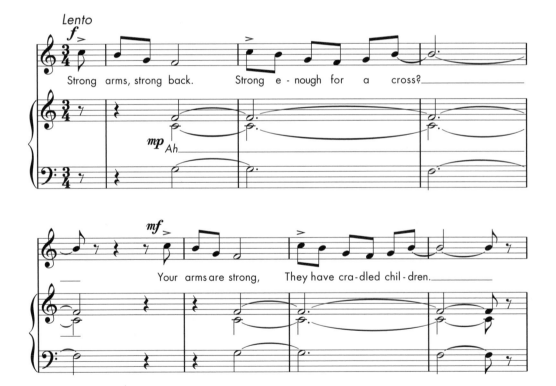

Kathy Galloway: words; Pat Livingstone: music

Jesus is stripped of his robe

Moderato

The si-lence is hot. They're all at-ten-tive now.___ The

Aah_____

sweat is stream-ing_____ The sweat is steam-ing_____ The flush is

ris-ing.___ The flesh is ris-ing.___ The eyes are shift-ing___

the eyes are drift-ing.___ The heat is sul-len.___

The threat is sul-len._____ Gripped, ripped, stripped.

Gripped, ripped, stripped.

Now you are rea-dy for ac-tion.

*Aah*_____

Kathy Galloway: words; Pat Livingstone: music

Jesus dies

Slow – haunting

sempre **mp**

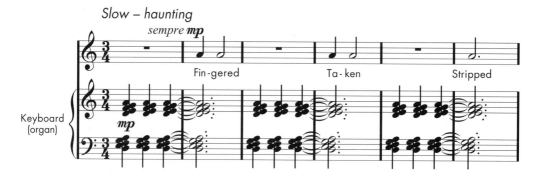

Fin-gered   Ta-ken   Stripped

Keyboard (organ)

mp

Kathy Galloway: words; Pat Livingstone: music

Jesus is taken from the cross

She will hold out her arms to you. She will take you up-on her knee. She will turn your face to her breast. She will rock you and sing gent-ly to you.

Kathy Galloway: words; Pat Livingstone: music

Holy Places 2004

Via Dolorosa

In the Old City
we read the inscriptions,
pause where a plaque on the wall
reminds us that Jesus falls
under the weight of the cross
over and over again.

In the refugee camp
we read the writing on the wall:
the stencilled images of martyrs,
graffiti, dusty posters,
calls to action, cries of pain
over and over again.

Women at the wall

At the Western Wall, women
hidden behind a wattle fence
reach across to touch
the scroll of the Law.

On the West Bank
there is another fence
topped with razor wire –

but there is no reaching over this barrier,
no appeal to the law that put it there.

Church of the Holy Sepulchre

All under one roof
like a religious shopping mall –
and as oppressive –
Calvary
and the Tomb
and the baffled common people

struggling up steps,
ducking through doorways,
lit by flickering lamps
each of which belongs
to a separate denomination.

A structure oppressive with power,
marked out into territories,
guarded by monks:
gloomy acres of space
patrolled by clergy in robes
and tour guides with worried flocks.

But what is at its heart?
Where would the people of God gather
who stray through the gloom
longing for meaning?

Such a pompous place,
such a weight of sadness,
so much history,
such disconnection
from what is happening in the streets –
such terrifying emptiness.

Why do we search for the living among the dead?

The flowers of the field

The poppy, the anemone –
blooming now after the spring rains –
they are different,
but both are as red as blood:

scattered across hillsides
where settlers' children play,
cared for by teachers carrying guns;

fragile among the rubble
where bulldozers groan
and fatherless children throw stones;

and when the wall is built,
they will still be flowering on both sides,
fragile as human lives –
different, but both as red as blood.

Jan Sutch Pickard

(These poems were written in 2004, when a small group from Scotland travelled as pilgrims to Jerusalem and the West Bank at the invitation of young people in Palestine.)

Why is he getting wrong? *

A child in the crowd watches Jesus carrying his cross through the streets of Jerusalem.

It's not fair!
Why is he getting wrong off the soldiers?
He's a good man.
Everyone knows him.

He helps people.
He makes them better.
He talks to people.
He tells stories – good stories.
Everybody listens to him.

Look at them!
Why are they hurting him?
Why won't they leave him alone?

He's not a bad man.
He's a kind man.
It's not fair.
Why is he getting wrong?

Ruth Burgess and Kirsty Langlands, aged 10

('Getting wrong' is a phrase used in the northeast of England and means 'getting into trouble' or 'getting blamed or punished'.)*

I don't understand adults

A boy in the crowd watches Jesus carry his cross.

I don't understand adults.
They make me angry sometimes.
Look at them now,
treating Jesus like a piece of dirt.
What has he done to be treated this way?

I met him once in our village.
His friends had been shouting at each other;
I'd watched them from the other side of the road.

Jesus called me over to him.
I was shy of strangers.
My mum had told me to be careful,
but I'd seen him before telling stories
and I'd listened to him.
He had some good ideas.

Jesus asked me what I enjoyed,
and I told him about the games I play with my friends.
He knew what I was talking about.
I told him about how I always got the blame when I row with my sister.
He knew about that too –
he'd had little sisters as well.

I like Jesus.
Grown-ups don't always listen to me
but I can talk to him,
and he listens and understands.

I feel sorry for him today.
I'm angry with the people who are hurting him.
And where are his friends?
Why aren't they sticking up for him?
Why have they all run away?

Ruth Burgess and Andrew Softley, aged 12

Seeing the face of Christ
(George's story)

Luke 24:13–16

I met George when I was going to college and working part-time at a shelter for homeless men. When I wasn't busy, and he was free, we'd sit and talk together, about art and classical music. As a young man, George had studied oil painting. He'd wanted to learn to draw like the old masters, he told me. He loved the art of portraiture especially, and had dreamed of, just once, capturing a face so that it 'mirrored the soul'.

At first it seemed a little surprising to be talking about art and music in the cacophony of a night shelter, surrounded by bare, nicotine-yellow walls and ugly, orange linoleum scarred with cigarette burns.

I'd heard that George had been a soldier, too, that he'd fought at Normandy and in the Desert campaign, later again in Korea, but when I asked him about that period of his life, he said he didn't like to talk about it.

Once when Tommy was having a seizure, and lay writhing on the cold floor like he'd been shot, I glanced up and saw George. He gazed down at Tommy and kept shaking his head; it was like he was away some place else. His face expressed infinite pity.

Blood drooled from the corner of Tommy's mouth; his body kept flailing and churning. 'Gonna be alright Tom,' said George. Tommy roiled and writhed, his boyish, trenched face contorted, tortured-looking. George handed me his suit jacket, balled-up for underneath Tommy's head. I tried to keep Tommy over on his side between attacks; with a tender, sore, caressing voice, George told Tommy that he was going to be all right, that he was just going to see the nurses. 'Just goin' to see the nurses,' the crowd of tough, scared men started up in a chorus. 'Tommy's just going to see the nurses.' 'Luck-y.' 'Some nice ones there, I'll bet ya.' 'Oh yeah, for sure.' 'Be alright now, Tommy.' 'Tommy, be alright.' And, finally, the ambulance screamed up with a stretcher the paramedics rolled Tommy on to like a bag of loose sticks.

My colleague Phil, who'd been working on the front line for years, and knew George better than anyone probably, said that George felt profound guilt for having survived the wars – that George couldn't understand why he'd lived when all his good friends, and so many other good people, had been blown away or left crippled for life, had been taken prisoner and tortured, had gone missing and never been found … He carried the question like a cross, Phil said.

'You see him alone sometimes, talking to himself, talking to God. Shouting at the heavens, praying for peace.'

A tabloid newspaper portrayed George as a dirty old drunk, on its front page one day. Some photo journalist shot him as he sat alone out on the front stoop of the shelter with a 'dead soldier' beside him.

He looked like a poor, pathetic soul: dressed in a crumpled tweed jacket, bowed down by heavy drink. The angle and light didn't do him justice, made his face look ugly and guttered. 'A Skidrow Alcoholic', the title underneath the picture read. There was a story concerning the growing number of homeless and the face of downtown. There was no report of him talking gently, humanly to Tommy as he lay writhing in hell, of the wars of liberation and absurdity he'd fought in through deserts and jungles and back streets; no mention that he had a wife and grown children somewhere, or of his dreams to become a fine artist who mirrored the soul.

No quote of him speaking knowledgeably, sensitively, passionately about the rich, beautiful, soaring music of Gustav Mahler.

The guys were mad. Somebody wanted to go down and teach the reporter a lesson. 'Give the poser a slashin'.'

Phil said it didn't surprise him. 'People have been painting him like that for ages now. Still hurt him though, I bet.'

George had one of the most beautiful faces I've ever seen. Sitting across from him one night, I told him that; I'd felt overwhelmed. He said thank you, that I was a gentleman.

It was hard to express with words. George's face was like grainy, grey rock, its features sculpted and etched by wind and rain, pocked and scarred by ice and snow; like an ancient landscape that had experienced fecund, young times of flowers; sudden rifts; slow, glacial change. George's face shone with the experience and wisdom of ages –

'Maybe that's what they mean,' said Phil. 'About suddenly seeing the face of Christ.'

Neil Paynter

People of the Passion

The soldier on duty

'Father, forgive them; they know not what they do.' (Luke 23:34)

Who the hell does he mean?
I ken fine what I'm doing.
Obeying orders, that's me.
'You're no paid to think, boy!
You've just to obey – and smartish!'
You join the army and that's it.

So if they say 'Crucify that man',
you bloody well crucify him – nae questions.
Well … you're saving a lot of lives.
After all, these so called Messiahs
stir up a lot of trouble,
and then we've to slaughter hundreds.

So crucifying one will maybe save a lot more.
Seeing what we do to Messiahs
will maybe teach them a sharp lesson.
You've got to be brutal with these people.
It's the only language they understand.
But I dinna like it all the same.

What's that? You're thirsty?
Of course you bloody well would be!
Well, chum, hae a drink on me.
Here's tae us … wha's like us?
Go on … sup it!

The priest

This young man from Galilee
has no idea of the tricky situation with Rome.
There is so much at stake.
I daresay he's a fine chap,
but what can he know?

You see ... it's a very delicate balance.
On one hand there is the worship. That's vital!
We have done a lot of negotiations
with the Romans.
They wanted a graven image of Caesar in the Holy of Holies.
That is unthinkable. 'No graven images!'

But we're always on a knife-edge here.
The important thing is
to keep the worship going,
to do the sacrifices properly
and dispense God's forgiveness responsibly.

That lunatic from Galilee was undermining this.
Little did he know of what is at issue here;
he was not aware of our careful dealings with Rome.
Yes, it's sad ... but we just had to get rid of him
before he brought the whole thing
down around our heads.

Thank God for Judas Iscariot,
he was a godsend.
Thanks to him we got it over quickly,
no fuss.

I always said that we could trust God
to find a way out of this mess.

The Pharisee

It was atrocious the way that Galilean
broke all the rules of the Law.
But we go by The Book – The Word of God.
Every rule and regulation must be observed carefully –
only that will save us.
Yet our supposed Messiah
was continually playing fast and loose with the Law.
Did you know that on several occasions he actually said:
'The Law of God says such and such.
But *I* say to you ...'

It's a wonder that God did not strike him dead on the spot.
Such arrogance provokes God's wrath.
Then he wonders why God has forsaken him!
What a nerve. We could tell him why.
He was a threat to Israel, undermining God's people.
So he had to go…
and there he goes now.

He's gone.
Now we can get on with proper religion.
Praise the Lord!
and pass the Bible.

Three poor bastards

There were three poor bastards: Robber 1, Robber 2 and the Man in the Middle.

As they crucified Rob1 and Rob 2, both of them used up all the curses and blasphemies they could – and they knew plenty!

But when it came to the man in the middle, he was strangely silent. He just lay down, spread out his arms and nodded to the soldiers as if to say, 'Get on with it.'

He never said a word, except: 'Father, forgive them; they don't know what they are doing.'

Yes! Even as those nails crunched through his wrists and ankles!

That made even Rob 2 think, in spite of his own torment.

Of course he'd seen the man in the middle healing and helping people. He had even befriended one or two of Rob 2's friends. *It hadn't done him much good, poor bastard*, thought Rob 2.

Then the soldiers came with the placards saying who they were … And over the man in the middle they put: 'King of the Jews'.

Oh bloody funny, thought Rob 2. *How damned Roman – making fun of the lot of us.*

The placard had a different effect on Rob 1: 'Go on, save yourself and us,' he screamed, along with a lot of other language which is unprintable.

'Och, shut up,' gasped out Rob 2. 'What the hell has he done to deserve this? We had it bloody coming to us, but him … he's done nothing wrong.' Then, after an agonising pause: 'Jesus … when you're King, remember me.'

Almost at once he knew it was a silly thing to say. He'd spent most of his life getting away from the authorities, hadn't he? Asking the king to remember him? *I must be daft*, he thought.

Then the man in the middle gasped out: 'Aye … I tell you … today… you'll be with me… in the Garden.'

A hellish hour passed and, as it did, Rob's life passed before him. He could see himself once more in the cave he had carved for himself, formed under the mountain of hurts which people had heaped on him as he grew up. It was miserable; but at least he knew what to do and did not expect anybody to help. They'd only let him down anyway, and make it worse.

'To hell with the lot of them' had become his motto. He made sure his cave was warmed by a fire of burning resentment against them all. But, of course, that fire had been eating away at the very foundations of his own life and that had just made him even angrier. It was their fault. Damn them all!

Then it all came back to him: how he used to pounce out on poor passers-by. He used to get satisfaction out of hurting them. If he was lucky there would be a few coins; and often he could grab something to flog to buy food and drink.

As the screams, sobs and curses of his victims came back to him, he knew now, only too well, what he had done … So the man in the middle was right. He had never really known what he was doing. What a trail of misery he'd left behind him. How could he face that terrible Judge of judges that the Bible speaks about?

Then the pain ebbed; the world became misty and fluid. There before him was a corridor leading up into the light. Gratefully he began to move up towards it, feeling so shabby. The mountain of hurts, with his cave inside it, was dissolving in the light. A gate opened and there he was in the Garden.

Somebody said gently: 'Why so surprised, pal? I told you, didn't I?' Rob gazed round and knew that the same voice was saying: 'I've got a special place ready for you in my Father's home. So, come on. You're not the only one who is dying to be loved and understood.'

The Roman centurion

Jesus said, 'I thirst.' A jar stood there full of sour wine; so they soaked a sponge, fixed it on a javelin and held it to his lips.

Gie the poor bastard a drink then!
How can he drink oot o a bottle?
Here, sir, hae a drink on me!
I'll dook this in my soor wine.
And here ye are … sup it!

My God, but you've got guts boy!
I've crucified a few in my time
but you're the daddy of them aa!
I ken I took the mickey oot o ye …
I wish I hadnae noo.
Aach, I'm a coarse bugger, I ken.

It'd been fine to hae a cup o wine together
before thon shower o priests got a haud of you.
Ye seem kinda … understandin … even stuck up there!
I thocht ye were just another criminal tae begin wi'
but I've fairly changed my tune.
Why the hell did they want tae crucify you?

You've no far to go noo, lad.
Death's your best friend when ye're on a cross.
He's no far awa noo.
But for what it's worth
ye've another friend here,
and there no a damn thing I can dae to help ye!
Sa bloody shame,
so it is.
Ach! Ye're the Son of a God all right,
so ye are!

The family

When Jesus saw his mother standing by, and the disciple he loved, he said: 'Lady, look! Your son.' And to the disciple: 'Look! Your mother.' (John 19:25–27)

Jesus,
my son, my dear son.
What have they done to you?
After all the people you healed!
How could they?
Why?!
Why?
Why didn't you come home when we came for you?
Your brothers, sisters and I.
We all saw that trouble was brewing.

If only Joseph had still been here,
he would have made sure you came home,
and then this wouldn't have happened.

But, yes, I'll take care of John,
though nobody can take your place,
not even John.

Yes, John, it's getting dark … I'll come.
But you must call me 'mum' now,
not Aunt Mary.

Ian Cowie

Good Friday in a northern town

God wasn't quite sure how she'd got into this position. To be sat on a rat-eaten armchair in a dark, rank back alley used for dumping rubbish was not a place anyone wanted to be, whether you're God or not. But, somehow, it seemed right. The only place she could be today. One thing she knew for certain: she'd wet herself. Cold and damp. Cold and damp against the pain of her legs. Pain everywhere. She wanted to wipe the mess and snot off her face and tried to raise her hand and head to meet each other. But it was too much and she let them fall. So she just sat there − a flabby bulk, prematurely aged, in a stained sack that might once have been a dress, and decayed sandals that were just the worst thing for this time of year. She tried to shout, but made hardly any sound and what sound there was made no sense. It was near the end.

Beyond the bin bags and boxes the world carried on. She could hear it − its busy self-concern echoed even here.

She remembered the look from the girl in the chicken shop yesterday − the look of one who cares, who knows you shouldn't judge, but who's paralysed with disgust and fear. The others were abusive and filled with contempt, saying she smelled; but the girl had wanted to act, to … and God had wanted to reach out and free her, but the time for action had passed.

It was the singing of birds she wanted most. She could have died for a blackbird's song, for just one of her children to take up the hymns she'd taught them at the world's birth. Instead, there was nothing but the city's vague industrial noise to counterpoint her lungs' labouring towards death. And the pigeon. The pigeon. God knows how long he'd been perched there (which God found quite funny, considering that she was God). But it hurt too much to laugh. The pigeon squatted uncomfortably on a melted wheelie bin, not wanting to get too close. He knew, you see; he'd worked out whom he was with. And he didn't like it one bit: In the midst of the filth and crap here was God. Filthy and unloved. Here she was, down here with the likes of the pigeons, the vermin, the scum and, for better or worse, it was as if she were one of them. It was too much for anyone to take in, let alone a pigeon, and he shuffled nervously to and fro, eyeing God with the cautious look of one who's had to dodge an aimed kick once too often. God didn't seem to mind – she just sat, lungs grating, slowly dying, gently watching the pigeon and glad of a friend. They waited a while.

Darkness was coming on. The pigeon sensed rain, but knew this was no time to run. Today there was no shelter to be found. Here was his place, exposed, with his God – exposed and alone. Time was up. God knew it, the pigeon knew it. It was finished and God thought again of the girl in the mall, and the mocking voices, and the gang of laughing drunken lads who'd beat her to a pulp last night, and was so filled with love that she could do nothing but die.

The pigeon could hold out no longer, and with all the grace he could muster (which wasn't a lot) flapped his way into the open, dead hand of God. And, somehow, in the midst of the rotten, hopeless scene, in a place the world would rather forget, he knew that today he was with God in Paradise.

Rachel Mann

He and she and we
(Words from the Cross, 2004)

When they came to the place that is called the Skull, they crucified Jesus there with the criminals, one on his right and one on his left. Then Jesus said, 'Father, forgive them; for they do not know what they are doing.' (Luke 23:33–34)

He was a Hutu.
The radio told him
that the Tutsis were like cockroaches
and must be destroyed –
he took his machete;
he went to his neighbour's house.
Father, forgive …

She sheltered her neighbours,
whose children had played with her children;
but then she became afraid for her own family –
she told them they must leave.
Father, forgive …

He was a priest.
The people gathered in his church
to pray for God's help and to beg for sanctuary;
his Archbishop reminded him of his duty –
he let in the soldiers.
Father, forgive …

He was a UN peacekeeper.
He saw what was happening;
he reported to people in offices far away;
they said 'Do nothing' –
his hands were tied.
Father, forgive …

She has shares
in a company that sold arms
to the government in Rwanda.
She heard the distant news;
the money still goes into her account.

And she and we must give account
for our complicity in the cruelty
and the cold violence of our world.
Father, forgive us …

Jan Sutch Pickard

At the cross

I see Christ crucified still – today:
where the hungry cry for food,
die for food,
though there's plenty.
Where people are yelled at,
jeered at –

bricks through their windows
because their skin isn't white, isn't right.
Where abuse and rape occur,
where gay men are beaten up,
where lust kills love –
I see him crucified still.

I see Christ crucified still – today:
where wars scar people, lands,
God's hands –
the endless, killing politics of hate.
Where the cry for justice
is unheard, oppressed, beaten down
by cold, world systems.
Where power comes first,
where religion twists faith,
where fear kills trust –
I see him crucified still.

I see Christ crucified still – today:
where creation's fabric shreds,
is bled,
by 'must have now', 'must use'.
Where earth's beauty is destroyed.
Where trees burn,
where water poisons,
where greed kills need –
I see him crucified still.

And I try – a little –
to stem the deadly tide
as I give – a little,
write to those in power – a little,
take my bottles to the bottle bank,
and try to love as he said;
try to love – a little.

O God, for all these crucifixions
may there one day be resurrection.

Chris Polhill

In your hands

Jesus gave a loud cry and said, 'Father into your hands I commit my Spirit.' And with these words he died. (Luke 23:46)

Christ died for us while we were yet sinning and that is God's own proof of his love for us. (Romans 5:8)

Praise be to God for the proof of his love for us.

Praise be to God that he has reconciled us to himself.

With Jesus we can say:
'Father, into your hands we commit our lives.'

In your hands our lives are safe, come what may.

We know that your forgiveness is greater than our sinfulness
and the bad side of us is in your hands.

Even though there may be difficulties and dangers ahead,
we are in your hands.

And when we pass through the valley of the shadow of death
we will pass through it fearing no evil,
knowing that you are with us,
and that we are in your loving hands.

Ian Cowie

Hope

You spoke of hope,
how we must identify with it –
be it for an unbelieving world.
Can you tell me how to live
that hope in Highgate*?
Can you bring that hope out of
the pulpit and explain it
so that those without money, without
jobs, without power, without
purpose can understand?
Can you tell me what hope there is
for kids whose parents are never
there when they need them,
for the old folk frightened to
walk to the shops,
for men and women whose jobs
have gone – and with them their dignity.
I read, long ago, that only a
suffering Christ makes sense.
Tonight the suffering of Highgate
is around me and in me
and a triumphant risen Christ is offensive,
for Highgate is an eternal Good Friday
and even Jesus broke down on the cross.
We are not ready for hope – not yet –
and some of us are not sure that we
will recognise it when it comes.

Ruth Burgess

*The Highgate in this poem is an area of Birmingham – another
place name could be substituted.*

Three prayers for Good Friday:

The denial of your image

Forgive us, Father,
for all the times we label others,
forgetting each one is made and loved by you.

Forgive us, Jesus,
for the little choices that blind us
to the pain we cause others to suffer.

Forgive us, Holy Spirit,
for silent collusion with systems
that deny justice and human need,
serve politics or convenience first.

Living God, forgive our inhumanity,
the denial of your image set within us;
pour your grace on this, our sorrow,
that we may find the courage to change
and honour your love for us. Amen

Our inhumanity

God forgive us for the inhumanity
that makes us bomb and blast
and see people as collateral damage.

God forgive us for the inhumanity
that imprisons, disappears or kills
those who do not fit our point of view.

God forgive us for the inhumanity
that makes slaves of other cultures
to put food and flowers on our table.

God forgive us for the inhumanity
that put Jesus on the cross.
And God forgive us
even when
we know what we do. Amen

Religious power abused

Jesus, our friend,
your death was contrived by the clergy,
twisting events to suit their needs.
So write your gospel on our hearts
that we yearn for justice by your laws.
And when we betray you to suit our needs,
may we hear the cock crowing,
turn towards your love
and try again to live your gospel
every day. Amen

Chris Polhill

God help us
(A meditation)

There is a time for asking questions
but there is also a day for decision.

There is a time to discuss who Jesus is,
but there is also a time to take up your cross and follow Him.

There is a time to weigh the issues carefully,
but there are issues which will not wait until tomorrow.

If we wait until we understand everything
we will wait for ever.

If we do not follow the light which we do see,
we will receive no more light.

If we, today, miss this opportunity
then God help us.

Ian Cowie

In the silence
(Prayers for Good Friday evening)

Lord God,
we meet beneath your cross this evening.
We meet –
friends, strangers, mourners –
grieving for the loss of love in the world.
We meet because we want to understand the awful things
that happened.
We meet because we want to be with you,
alongside you on your cross.

And in our meeting, we keep silence.
We keep silence in a time when words fail us.
We keep silence as you kept silence on the cross.
And so we keep silence with those crucified today,
with those who live in darkness, in despair, in pain.

We keep silence with those treated as today's scapegoats:
lone parents, gay men, lesbian women, loners,
people who seem different, strange …

Silence

We keep silence with those robbed of a sense of belonging in our society: women beaten up by money-lenders, mothers whose sons have been murdered …

Silence

We keep silence with the folk of Belfast – Loyalists and Republicans – and all who march through that city's streets this weekend.

Silence

We keep silence with all who mourn a loved one.

Silence

We keep silence with those rebuilding their lives in places of conflict.
Their names are out of the headlines but the slaughter still goes on.

Silence

We keep silence with those known to us today who live in darkness.
Who find it hard to see beyond death and desolation and despair.

Silence

In the pain, misfortune, oppression and death of the people,
God is silent.
God is silent on the cross
in the crucified.
And this silence is God's word, God's cry.
In solidarity, God speaks the language of love.

Ruth Harvey

Leading home the child of God

Father, we thank you for the angel of death;
putting an end to earthly torment,
delivering the tortured from the torturer,
freeing the prisoner from the prison,
leading home the child of God.

Ian Cowie

Holy Saturday

We wait in hope

God of life and death
WE WAIT IN HOPE.

God of all the worlds that are
WE WAIT IN HOPE.

God of dazzling darkness[3]
WE WAIT IN HOPE.
WE WAIT IN HOPE AND AWE.

Ruth Burgess

Conversations in a graveyard

John Miller, a minister in Glasgow, once shared a story with me of an afternoon he
spent in a graveyard:

'I'd heard that every year the Roman Catholic churches hold a mass in the local
cemetery,' he said. 'Apparently this mass at the burial place is a custom among the
Irish. I've been the minister of this Church of Scotland parish for thirty years and a
year or two ago I went along to the service myself. In a crowd of several hundred I
found myself standing among many people I knew. Some were my neighbours. With
others I had shared in a family funeral. After the mass everyone strolled from grave to
grave, talking fondly to other families, laughing at good memories, asking after one
another with genuine concern.

'The afternoon was extremely moving. With heightened emotions people shared
their thoughts about life and death, about family and loss, and about the Kingdom of
Heaven and the resurrection.'

Holy Saturday is traditionally the time when graves are tended in preparation for
Easter Sunday. Maybe on Holy Saturday, the place of burial is a good and meaning-
ful place to be.

Ruth Burgess and John Miller

Always

My father was good at loving,
had a lifetime's practice
loving friends, strangers, puss cats,
anyone who crossed his path.
Chiefly, and dutifully, he worshipped God
and he loved us, his family.
I, who am less experienced in such matters,
cannot begin to reckon his sum,
but he told us often that he loved us.
'Now and always' and I believed him.
Still do. Utterly.

Frances Copsey

Turning the ashes

In some cemeteries, gardens of remembrance and graveyards, cremated ashes are scattered in a specific area of ground. This is a liturgy to accompany an annual event when the ashes scattered throughout the year are turned into the earth.

Opening responses:

Dust to dust, ashes to ashes
FROM GOD WE CAME, TO GOD WE RETURN

In God we live, in God we have our being
FROM GOD WE CAME, TO GOD WE RETURN

We are part of a cycle of living and dying
FROM GOD WE CAME, TO GOD WE RETURN

In God we die, in God we go on living
FROM GOD WE CAME, TO GOD WE RETURN

Words to be said as the earth is turned:

Matter to matter
Ashes to ashes
Dust to dust
WE TURN THIS EARTH

Diggers and burrowers
Gardeners and growers
Ploughers and furrowers
WE TURN THIS EARTH

Spring to summer
Summer to harvest
Harvest to hibernation
WE TURN THIS EARTH

Turn us God
Turn us with the seasons
Turn us with the generations
TURN US WITH THE EARTH

Words of remembrance

(to be said after people have had the opportunity to think about and talk about those who have died):

All our laughter, all our sadness
SAFE NOW IN GOD'S HANDS

All our anger, all our gladness
SAFE NOW IN GOD'S HANDS

All our stories, all our memories
SAFE NOW IN GOD'S HANDS

Those we remember, those we love
SAFE NOW IN GOD'S HANDS

Closing responses:

We travel on
from birth to dying
WE ARE GOING HOME

We travel on
from dying to living
WE ARE GOING HOME

We travel on
through pain and laughter
WE ARE GOING HOME

We travel on
with hope and wonder
WE ARE GOING HOME

Suggested songs:

'We belong to God' (from *One is the Body*, Wild Goose Resource Group, Wild Goose Publications)

'Dust, dust and ashes' (see below)

Suitable Bible readings:

John 12:24
Genesis 3:19
Ecclesiastes 3:1–8
Romans 8:38–39
Psalm 90:1,6,12,14,16,17
Psalm 103:13–18

Dust, dust and ashes

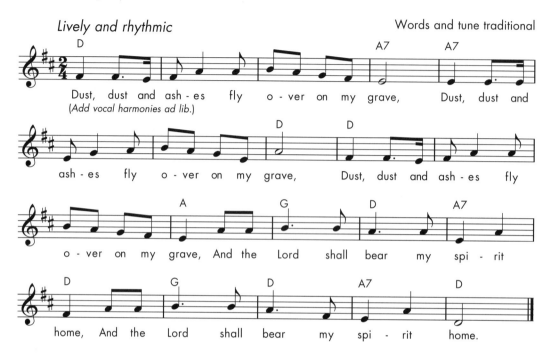

Lively and rhythmic   Words and tune traditional

Dust, dust and ash-es fly o-ver on my grave, Dust, dust and
(Add vocal harmonies ad lib.)
ash-es fly o-ver on my grave, Dust, dust and ash-es fly
o-ver on my grave, And the Lord shall bear my spi-rit
home, And the Lord shall bear my spi-rit home.

The tune has two variations to carry the verses:

Variation one, verses 2,3,5,6

They cru-ci-fied my Sa-viour, and nailed Him to the cross

Variation two, verses 4 and 7

He rose [He rose] He rose [He rose] He rose__ from the dead,

Dust, dust and ashes fly over on my grave,
And the Lord shall bear my Spirit home.

They crucified my Saviour, and nailed him to the cross
And the Lord, etc.

O Joseph begged his body, and laid him in the tomb
And the Lord, etc.

He rose, He rose, He rose from the dead,
And the Lord, etc.

O Mary came a-running her saviour for to see
And the Lord, etc.

The Angels said , 'He's not here, he's gone to Galilee'
And the Lord, etc.

He rose, He rose, He rose from the dead
And the Lord, etc.

Dust, dust and ashes fly over on my grave.
And the Lord, etc.

Not beyond my ken (Psalm 131)

Music: Panmure Courante/After the Paunges of a Desperate Lover (traditional)

Introduction: I, instrumentally

1. O Lord, arrogance I abhor,
   And never let my lip betray pride and sclore.*

2. In quietness my soul I've put to rest.
   I do not aspire to things beyond my ken.

3. Tranquil my soul that I set within your peace, Lord.
   Deep in your peace like a child upon the breast.

4. Touching not clinging, my freedom you awaken.
   God, your covenant love will invite me to adore.

(Repeat verses 1 and 2; then 3, 4, and 1 instrumentally. End with verse 2.)

da Noust

*sclore: Scots for gossip (or substitute scorn)

The Easter vigil

Wait and see
(Opening responses for an Easter vigil)

Voice 1:   Jesus has died and Jesus is buried. Lord, where shall we go?
ALL: LORD, WHERE SHALL WE GO?

Voice 2:   Jesus is dead and hope is smothered. Lord, where shall we go?
ALL: LORD, WHERE SHALL WE GO?

Voice 3:   Jesus has died and darkness triumphs. Lord, where shall we go?
ALL: LORD, WHERE SHALL WE GO?

Voices 1, 2, 3: Jesus has died but dawn is breaking.
                Let us stay and watch and pray.

ALL: FOR GOD IS LOVE.
                LOVE HOPES ALL THINGS.
                WITH GOD ALL THINGS CAN COME TO BE;
                NEW LIFE CAN COME THROUGH JESUS.

Voice 1:   But Jesus has died and Jesus is buried.

Voice 2:   But Jesus is dead and hope is smothered.

Voice 3:   But Jesus has died and darkness triumphs.

Voices 1, 2, 3: But wait … and wait … and wait … and see.

ALL: WE SHALL WAIT AND WE SHALL SEE.

David Coleman

Prayers for the Easter vigil:

At the lighting of the new fire

On this holy night,
the wounded Christ
offers hope.

The lighting of the Easter candle

Come, liberating Christ,
rise to meet us!
Hear our wounded cries
in the travail of the earth;
banish the darkness of
our fears;
release us
from the tomb
of powerlessness
into empowered
living
in the light
of your liberation.

Liturgy of renewal

As we celebrate the resurrection of Jesus Christ,
we give thanks for the promise of Christ to be with us always.
Christ with us
in our birthing,
our living,
our dying.

Through our observance of Lent,
we have reflected on God's gift of life.
We now recall our baptism in Christ,

giving thanks for the waters of birth,
play,
refreshment,
cleansing,
life-giving.

Mindful of our baptismal commitment
to turn to Christ,
to repent of our sins,
to renounce evil,
we recommit ourselves
to do justly,
love mercy
and walk humbly with our God.

As we place these lights in the water,
we renew our baptismal commitment.

(Candles are floated in the font.)

WE TURN TO CHRIST
IN THE LOVE
BETWEEN US,
THE PASSION
WITHIN US,
THE UNEXPECTED
INSPIRING US,
AND THE EARTH'S EMBRACE.

WE REPENT OF OUR SOLIDARITY IN THE SIN OF THE WORLD,
ACKNOWLEDGING THAT WITHIN US WHICH WOUNDS OTHERS.

WE COMMIT OURSELVES TO
WORKING FOR CHANGE AND HEALING
IN OURSELVES AND THE WORLD.

WE COMMIT OURSELVES TO WISDOM
IN NAMING EVIL,
COURAGE
TO EXPOSE IT,

AND STRENGTH
FOR PUTTING LIBERATION
INTO ACTION.

God of life-giving water,
we pray for all harmed by water exploitation, pollution, drought and flood:
for all living in squalor, devastation and fear;
for women and children who travel daily to carry water home;
for those whose lives are risked on the seas;
for all who depend on others for a cup of water;
for all who work towards the justice of clean water for everyone.
God of life-giving water,
hear our prayer.

Blessing of the Easter garden

Risen Christ,
as Mary Magdalene met you in the resurrection garden,
so may we meet you
in this sacred space
of birthing, growth
and hope.

With you we bless this garden,
the gardens around us,
and the earth we care for.
Bless those who prepared this garden,
those who tend the gardens of this house (village/town/city)
and all who enjoy them.

Through the gifts you have given,
inspire us to live the resurrection
through our responsibility to the earth.

Elizabeth Baxter

Brighten this holy night

Light of life,
giver of all good gifts,
through your unfolding story
our stories unfold.
In calling us to drink
when we are thirsty
you empower us for our task
to heal the nations.
Brighten this holy night
by your star,
that in the morning
we may meet you
risen again. Amen

Elizabeth Baxter

Thanks be to you
(prayers of thanksgiving)

May God be with you,
AND ALSO WITH YOU.
Lift up your hearts,
WE LIFT THEM UP TO GOD.
Let us love the Lord, our God, with all our heart and all our soul and all our might,
IT IS RIGHT TO GIVE OUR THANKS AND PRAISE.

Thanks be to you, God awesomely distant.
Thanks for the searing of shooting stars,
the colours of the planets in the night sky,
the space and power beyond our perceiving,
which sparkles the sky of our lives with your caring.

Thanks be to you God, uncomfortably close,
giving life to dead, dry things.
Both the dance of pure stillness
and the beat of our hearts are your doing.

And thanks be to you, God known in a body,
who blessed as he lived,
who raised up our lives
to be gathered as one,
reaching out for the kingdom.
Born of Mary, he shares our life.
Eating with sinners, he welcomes us.
Guiding his children, he leads us.
Visiting the sick, he heals us.
Dying on the cross, he saves us.
Risen from the dead, he gives us new life.

Sanctus

Holy, holy, holy,
vulnerable God,
heaven and Earth are full of your glory.
HOSANNA IN THE HIGHEST

Blessed is the one who comes in God's name.
HOSANNA IN THE HIGHEST

Prayer after communion

God of truth in love,
you gave us eyes and we have seen;
you gave us hands and we have touched.
Christ, our risen and intimate lover and brother,
we have taken you into our bodies
so that we may be transformed,
so that we may grow in faith and in love for you
as we meet you in each other.
AMEN

David Coleman

Easter Sunday

The first gold of dawn

The long day
stretched into night
and time crept onward
towards the new day.

With the first gold of dawn
came a resurrection,
a new hope that grew
with the rising sun,
and went out to a waiting world.

Jean Murdoch

God has made laughter for us

Christ is risen; He is risen indeed. Alleluia!

Risen in quiet and mysterious darkness
before the chorus of the dawn.
Alleluia, Christ is risen;
HE IS RISEN INDEED.

Risen with glory and grace in reserve,
and authority beyond measure.
Alleluia, Christ is risen;
HE IS RISEN INDEED.

Risen to prove that violence is no solution;
to offer us peace and life in all its fullness.
Alleluia, Christ is risen;
HE IS RISEN INDEED.

For God has taken into his own flesh
the sin of the world.
The last laugh is God's laugh;
God has the last laugh:
For freedom comes beyond the cross,
for peace comes beyond the violence,

for friendship comes beyond the betrayal.
For life comes beyond the crushing of life.

The first laugh and the last laugh are God's.
And God has made laughter for us.
Alleluia, Christ is risen;
HE IS RISEN INDEED.

David Coleman

Easter celebration from Holy Rood House

The gathering

In this moment
we are gathered
welcoming love's
return

OUR HEARTS ARE LIFTED
WE OPEN OUR EYES
WE WELCOME LOVE

the tomb is empty
the stone laid back

THE WOMB IS FULL
THE STONES CRY OUT
FOR JOY.

Risen One,
stand among us
speak your words of peace
release us from our fears
heal us from our wounds

FORGIVE OUR BETRAYALS,
OUR DENIALS OF YOUR LOVE,
THAT WE MAY PARTICIPATE IN YOUR JUST LIVING.

Holy dancer,
you soar from the grave
with cosmic rhythm,
wiping earth's tears
in heralding the dawn

HOLD OUR HANDS
IN THE DANCE OF JUSTICE
WEAVE OUR STEPS INTO SPIRALS OF FREEDOM.

The ministry of the Word

As storytellers
we shape your
unfolding story

as passionate people
we share your
passion for justice

as bearers of God
we embody your life
in the world

HUMBLE US TO LISTEN
TO FORGOTTEN STORIES

EMPOWER US WITH BOLDNESS
WHEN WE ARE AFRAID

RE-SOURCE US
FOR THE BIRTHING OF LIBERATION

Intercessions

With resurrection hope and action we bring our prayers …

The peace

Jesus stood among his disciples and said, 'Peace be with you; why are you frightened, and why do doubts arise in your hearts? Look at my hands and my feet. Touch me and see.'

Invitation to the table

Gather around this resurrection table where all are welcomed and the good earth is affirmed. From her generosity, we bring these gifts of bread and wine.

WITNESSES TO HOPE,
WE PARTICIPATE
IN CHRIST'S LIBERATION.

Eucharistic prayer

Be still
and know that I am God.

WE ARE STILL IN YOUR PRESENCE
YOU ARE STILL WITH US.

In Christ you accompany us,
embodied among us,
sharing our birthing
our living
our dying

SHARING OUR DREAMS OF HOPE AND LIBERATION,
OFFERING US NEW LIFE
AND THE SHATTERING
OF THE TOMB.

In Christ
you appear as the host
at the ebbing and the flowing of our lives

YOU BECKON US TO SHARE YOUR HOSPITALITY,
YOUR CHALLENGE OF LOVE.

In Christ
you sit as the guest
at the table of the stranger

YOU BLESS US WITH YOUR PRESENCE,
YOUR AWAKENING OF LOVE.

In Christ
you stand among us
as host and guest at the heart of this community

YOU SHARE WITH US YOUR VULNERABILITY,
YOUR UNWRAPPING OF LOVE.

As hosts with Christ,
we bless this bread.

As guests with Christ,
we pour this wine.

As welcomed strangers,
united in Christ's life, death, and embodied liberation,
we hear the words of promise:

This is my body given for you;
take and eat to re-member me.

This cup poured out:
this is the new covenant in my blood;
take and drink to re-member me.

In this action of justice-making,
we recall
broken minds and bodies
and blood shed through lust for power
and nature's turn of hand.

RESTORE AND HEAL
ALL THAT IS WOUNDED

BE PRESENT
IN THE STILLNESS
OF THE WAITING

ROLL BACK THE STONE
OF PREJUDICE
AND FEAR

RELEASE THE SIGNS
OF SPRING.

Breaking of bread

We gently break this bread
of fragile life

OUR BREAKING DOWN
BECOMES OUR BREAKING THROUGH.

As we eat this living bread
and drink the new wine of resurrection,
let us celebrate the cosmic Christ,
our liberator and sustainer

WITH DIVINE TENDERNESS
YOU REMAKE US

BY TRANSFORMING PAIN
YOU HEAL US –

YOUR PASSIONATE ENERGY
EMPOWERS US.

Sharing of bread and wine

Blessing

God
source of our life
bless with boldness
caress with care

Christ
Wisdom of God
bless with boldness
caress with care

Spirit
midwife of new beginnings
bless with boldness
caress with care. Amen

Elizabeth Baxter

This is the Good News
(Easter affirmation)

This is the Good News –
The grave is empty,
Christ is risen.
HALLELUJAH!

This is the Good News –
The light shines in the darkness,
and the darkness can never put it out.
HALLELUJAH!

This is the Good News –
Once we were no people,
now we are God's people.
HALLELUJAH!

Christ is our peace,
the indestructible peace
we now share with each other.

We gather in God's name
(Easter responses from Iona)

We have travelled a long way to come here,
from many places, and through Holy Week to Easter.
NOW WE GATHER IN GOD'S NAME IN GOD'S PLACE.

We have told the story of Jesus's suffering and death,
and remembered how the disciples were scattered in despair.
NOW WE CELEBRATE CHRIST RISEN FROM THE DEAD.

We have been silent in the face of failure and fear;
but now have found our voices, know your hope.
NOW WE SHOUT THE GOOD NEWS, SING ALLELUIA.

Lead us Lord
(Easter responses from Iona)

Lord of life, you walk this journey with us and through us;
LEAD US LORD, LEAD ON.

Journeying within, and wrestling with the world,
LEAD US LORD, LEAD ON.

Lead us to risk, to grow, and to tread the path you have opened for us;
LEAD US LORD, LEAD ON.

And let us rejoice that every place is your place;
IN THE NAME OF CHRIST, THE RISEN ONE. AMEN

The Sabbath day was over
(Easter morning song)

The Sabbath day was over, and through the grey of dawn
The women crept in silence, bewildered and forlorn,
To find the borrowed grave where their Master had been laid
And offer love's last homage although they were afraid.

The tomb was broken open, the guard had fled away,
The empty grave-clothes gleamed in the rising light of day.
The body had been taken, no knowing why or how;
The spices and sweet ointments had lost their purpose now.

A stranger told the news that as yet they could not see:
'The Crucified is living, he waits in Galilee.
Go tell his friends to follow; speak out, be not dismayed!'
They ran, but spoke to no one, because they were afraid.

By mystery of your Spirit you gave their message voice,
The dumb were made to speak and the grieving to rejoice;
For somewhere on their journey in truth they met with you:
From death and dread and silence the word of life broke through.

We fear your resurrection, unfathomable Lord;
To follow you will cost us more than we dare afford.
But yet the Gospel fires us: the price of love is paid,
And we will not keep silence – though we are still afraid.

Mark 16:1–8

Liz Varley

Suggested Tunes: Aurelia or Sprowston

God is on the loose
(from an Easter sermon)

Reading: Mark 16:1–8

The account of the resurrection that we've just heard from Mark's gospel was probably the first one to be written down. It's seldom if ever read nowadays on Easter Sunday, because of the way it ends. After the women come to the tomb, find it empty and meet the mysterious stranger with his shattering news, Mark simply writes, 'So they went out and ran from the tomb, distressed and terrified. They said nothing to anyone, for they were afraid.'

Small wonder, you may think, that this is not often read on Easter Sunday. Today is meant to be a day of joy and gladness – and here is Mark giving us a picture of distress, of fear, of terror! No, we prefer John's account or Luke's – they hit the more suitable notes of wonder and celebration. What is there to be afraid of, after all, on this day of resurrection?

What is there to be afraid of? Well, perhaps there was good reason for the fear that overcame these women, for with the resurrection the pattern of life and death was broken – for ever. With the resurrection not only is this pattern blown wide open, now all that happens in life requires to be reviewed. For if God has broken even the bonds of death, then all dying, from whatever cause and however tragic, is nevertheless not the final word on us human beings. Paul's great cry of triumph: 'Death, where is thy sting? Grave, where is thy victory?' now surely applies to every death – and offers the possibility of a totally new approach to the whole of life from now on.

That is frightening.

But perhaps there is another reason to be afraid. And perhaps we would do well to pause and consider it for a moment. Maybe we can put it this way: Watch out! God is on the loose. God is out of the box!

You see, when you think about it, haven't we human beings always tried to keep God in a box, under our control? We've tried to keep God in the box of religion. We have allowed ourselves to be persuaded that God can be subjected to rules and regulations and religious practices, can be under the control of religious hierarchies, church committees, human systems. Do this, and God will be pleased with you; do that, and we can assure you that you will fall under God's severe displeasure. Isn't that the way, very often, that religious bodies imagine they control God?

But believe in resurrection and God is free, free from all religious systems, free to use religion to meet us on God's terms. As Jesus told us, 'The wind blows wherever it wishes; you hear the sound it makes, but you do not know where it comes from or where it is going. It is like that with everyone who is born of the Spirit.' (*Good News Bible*)

So perhaps there is reason to be a little afraid, as we look at the empty tomb: To be afraid that our attempts to control God through religion are doomed; to be afraid that our cherished traditions are, in fact, not the last word, for God has had the last word – or rather we should maybe say the last laugh, that mighty laugh of God's life as God broke free from every bond on that first Easter Day. God is on the loose! Tremble then, all who think they have God tied down with religion.

And if God is free – if Christ is risen – then there can, in fact, be no forcing of God into any human box at all. Not only can we no longer think that God is a Protestant or a Catholic, or white, black or brown; no longer think that God is more like us nice middle class folk; no longer imagine that God prefers Christians to Muslims or vice versa. Now we can no longer allow any ideology or nation to hijack God. God is not on 'our' side any more than God is on 'their' side. So tremble, you statesmen and women who imagine you can co-opt God onto your side or into your army or into your ideological box. God can never again be tied down by any of our political systems, however wonderful we may imagine them to be. God is on the loose.

And I suspect – indeed I am increasingly convinced – that to truly celebrate the resurrection, to truly welcome God on the loose, we need to be constantly willing to hand over control to God. All must be constantly handed over, laid down, given up, and we must allow God to be God: crucified and risen and on the loose in our world, out of our control.

So, I like the way Mark tells the story. I like the way he doesn't try to pretty it up, or analyse it, or make it fit any of our preconceptions. I like the picture of these women and their fear. And I like the thrill of imagining the unimaginable: the One who made the sun, the moon and the stars bursting out not just from the tomb, but from every box into which we try to put him, and striding free and majestic and totally out of our control, into all our lives; inviting, challenging, summoning us to be free – like him!

John Harvey

Tell them how much we love them

(This prayer might be said around the family table, at Easter breakfast or lunch, between courses.)

We remember today, those we love who have died:

(Those present share names, stories, photos, mementos of family members, friends, pets …)

We remember (say name, light candle) who …

Tell them, God, how much we love them,
how much we miss them.
Tell them we carry their stories in our lives.

Today we rejoice that Jesus lived and died and is risen.
Today we trust you, Jesus, that there is life after death
and that you will always be with us,
loving us and leading us home.

Glory be to God,
Creator, Redeemer, and Holy Spirit. Amen

Alternative Gloria

God be with us day by day.
Jesus, join us in our play.
Holy Spirit, be our friend
now and evermore. Amen

Tune: Buckland ('Thank you for the world so sweet')

Ruth Burgess

It took tough love
(from Night Shelter)

Isaiah 43:1–4

It was my job to ask anybody new their name. There was a tough-looking young man shovelling sugar on his bowl of cold cereal. I went over and introduced myself. He didn't answer, or look up. When I asked him his name he told me to fuck off.

The next night, I approached him again.

He growled, and said his name was Donald. When I asked him his surname, his hands clenched into fists.

'Duck,' he said.

Although he made me want to keep a safe distance, I'd try to make some contact when he came into the shelter. I'd offer him something to eat. I'd ask about the weather.

It was some time before we had our first true conversation:

'Fuckin' brilliant dumplings,' he said one night, 'these home-made?' He tried another spoonful and his dead eyes lit up. 'So who made these?' he asked, and glanced round.

I sat down beside him.

He told me he'd lived with his granny when he was a boy, and that she would make him beef stew with dumplings.

'Brilliant,' he sang, digging in.

It took a long time before he really opened up.

It took the homey smell of Norman's cooking.

It took people remembering his name, and giving him a warm welcome when he trudged in from the cold.

It took Ray's knock-knock jokes.

It took straight talk.

It took Sue finding him clean clothes and a decent, warm coat.

It took a long time.

Then, one summer evening, he told me his story:

We were sitting out on the church steps. He told me that he was a professional chef and had worked in a restaurant downtown. He'd worked his way up, but then lost his job when the place went bust. After that, he lost his flat and started sleeping on the streets.

He nursed a tall can of Strong Brew – he was rattling, he said, and took a hit; the pale inside of his arm was bruised and marked.

I asked him what sort of food he'd cooked and he said he could cook anything and everything, but that cakes were his speciality.

'That's my real talent. Layer cakes, cheesecakes, sponges. Birthday cakes, wedding cakes – you name it.'

I thought of this tough, hard man baking cakes: the strong hands that had looked like they wanted to strangle the life out of me, squeezing out thick icing; piping beautiful rosettes. I thought of the hard work and patience needed, the skill and artistry.

He wanted to start his own business, he told me. His own business selling cakes – cakes by mail order, cakes on the Internet; that was his dream, he said, and shrugged.

I thought of a cake falling. 'No, why don't you?' I said.

He took another hit of Strong Brew, then told me about the time a famous food critic visited the restaurant. At the end of the meal the critic asked to shake the hand of the person who had made the raspberry soufflé, and he got called out.

'You must have felt proud,' I said.

'I felt brilliant,' he answered, sitting, working the empty crushed can.

He started to give us a hand around the night shelter, running boxes and crates into the kitchen whenever there was a delivery or donation.

Another evening out on the steps he told me that he had a five-year-old son.

I asked him his son's name and he said: 'Rory.'

His son was in care. His girlfriend was in detox. (I imagined him for a moment, back in the world of birthdays and weddings.) He'd been on the streets two years in September, he said, and fell silent.

'Rory, that's a beautiful name,' I told him.

It took a long time to build trust.

It took Ray who'd lived on the streets and was a counsellor now.

It took Ray and Jane and Tony and people who had been there.

It took people who had never been there exactly but who could empathise.

It took Ann mothering him when he was sick, and people treating him like a human being again.

It took accepting him at the door, drunk and difficult and out of his head.

It took us barring him for a week for throwing an empty plate and calling Rahim, 'Paki bastard'.

It took tough love.

It took Father William's understanding, gentle way.

It took giving him a home address so he could finally get a paybook sent.

It took a long time.

Then one night he told us that his name wasn't Donald, by the way. It was Brendon. 'Brendon Matthewson,' he pronounced, and watched me write his name down in the book.

'Here,' he said and took the pen.

I wondered if it was a sign – a sign he was growing more accepting of himself, that he was ready to begin dealing with his past, and future?

'Brendon. It suits you,' I said.

He smiled.

He became protective of us. One night when someone was giving Ann a rough time on the door, he came out and told the guy to show the woman some respect – that, or he'd be out on his arse; it was his choice, he told him.

As the months passed he seemed to be feeding his addictions less; there was a mischievous glimmer in his eyes – he traded jokes with Ray, recipes with Norman. You weren't always reaching out to him: down a long deep depression, inside of a black hole.

Then one day he told us we probably wouldn't be seeing him for a while. There was a warrant with his name on it, he explained. 'Can't keep your head down for ever,' he said, and walked up the road to the cop shop.

Ray and Jane visited him.

When he got out, he landed a job cooking in the shelter kitchen. He wanted to give something back, he said.

'Fuckin' brilliant,' all the guys raved. He was teaching Norman some things.

On Christmas day, he and Stormin' served-up an awesome and legendary feast: turkey with all the trimmings; roast potatoes; brussels sprouts; chipolata sausages and rolled bacon; and for dessert, out of this fuckin' world Christmas pudding topped with cream and brandy butter.

Brendon said his plan was to save his wages and get some gear together – piping bags, tubes, syringes, a decent set of knives and spoons.

Three years later, he stopped me in the street. He called my name and I turned around. I didn't recognise him at first. 'Brendon!' I cried.

He looked like a different person. He looked brand new.

It was a bright warm spring day and we shared our news:

He was a pastry chef at Costco supermarket, he told me; he was in charge of cake decoration and of interviewing and training bakery staff. He was living with his wife, Jamila, and his stepdaughter, Sara, in a little house outside the city.

He'd been through some ups and downs – rehab twice. It hadn't been easy. He told me about trying to go cold turkey, about the hunger pain of withdrawal.

He was feeling brilliant now. Life was sweet. Jesus Christ had called him, he revealed – and proudly, soberly showed me his tattoo of a Celtic cross. His arms were hard with muscles – cook's arms – sinewy from the push and pull of hard work, clean except for a couple recent burn marks from the oven.

It was the last time I saw Brendon.

I think of him sometimes: icing names onto birthday cakes in the brilliant light of Costco; living in a house with his wife, Jamila, and stepdaughter, Sara.

Neil Paynter

Maggie's teeth

2 Corinthians 5:1–2

'Maggie, you've got your teeth!'

Maggie stands and smiles, modelling them for us. 'Madonna, eat your heart out,' she says, and laughs in her husky, earthy way.

It's quite a contrast: the false perfection of the new, white-white teeth against the brown, wrinkled background of her crooked, beaten face.

It only took a year. 'Wait for your cheque.' 'Wait for your teeth.' Maggie has learned patience. (Like everybody here in the night shelter, she's had to.) She knows it takes a long, long time for anything to trickle down to a shelter in a basement.

Maggie accepts she is decaying, knows parts waste away – genitals, minds. Having no teeth is a trial, but after so many trials and losses – abusive men, dead-end jobs, poor housing and rich landlords, psychiatrists and social workers, breast cancer; a best friend who lost all hope; a good friend who was murdered – you learn to endure, and to live with little things like having no teeth.

'You really look great, Mags,' I say, setting up for bingo.

'Well, thank you dear, but they're just a plug in a leak, you know. The body dies, the soul is eternal, as they say. But at least I can chew now, no more soup and mush,' she says, and smiles brightly again.

'Alleluia,' I answer, and stop and gaze at her. But it's not her new white-white teeth I'm struck by – although I'm very happy she finally has them – it's her old laughing eyes – and the light that has never left her. The beautiful, strong light that no one has been able to blacken, or rob, or put out, or take away – that no force can kill. The miraculous, amazing light she has, somehow, never lost faith in.

After bingo, Maggie invites us out for fish and chips with the gang – with Bill and Kate and Dagmar and Doreen – to celebrate Kate's birthday and her new teeth.

Neil Paynter

Symbols of resurrection

We have made a resurrection garden as a part of our gardens on the theme of the Christian spiritual journey. It was the hardest to make because resurrection gets so little time in our church life; Lent and Holy Week receive plenty of attention, but resurrection? A nod on Easter Day and then, generally, the great fifty days of Easter are ignored. So it was a challenge to express resurrection.

The first space is a Mary Magdalene garden, made enclosed yet open by having a circle of upright posts as a boundary. There is a stone (the stone rolled away) with a tree of heaven by it. We grow a few vegetables, and have some old tools in the garden – a spade and a wheelbarrow – as Mary mistook Jesus for the gardener. On the yellow brick path is creeping thyme, and, close by, other sweet-smelling plants like the winter-flowering honeysuckle and camomile lawn, because Mary brought sweet-smelling herbs to the tomb. There is an almond tree in the centre of the garden, associated with Mary Magdalene because of the sound of its name in Greek, *amygdalus*. We have also planted a Mary Magdalene rose, which has a scent like myrrh.

The next area is a story-telling place to encourage people to tell their own resurrection stories. This is set underneath a hazel tree with two benches. As part of the floor between the benches there are two lines of tiles with an interweaving Celtic pattern – interweaving like our life experiences, of sorrow and joy, dark and light. The joy of Easter is not the surface joy of a party, but the joy that only comes through suffering, the joy that comes when God's perspective makes a new pattern of suffering. A resurrection pattern that does not deny the suffering but alters its perspective.

Hung in the story-telling place are butterflies, some made of CDs by a youth group, and others made from glass picked up off the streets of Bethlehem after Israeli tanks had rumbled through – butterflies made by Palestinians as a prayer for the resurrection of their country.

Then there are a few coppiced trees. When you coppice a tree for fuel it grows again and again.

Next are 'surprise beds'. Alternately these have wheat – another symbol of resurrection – and flowers grown from seeds given to visitors. Visitors don't know what kinds of seeds they have been given to plant and, later in the year, get the nice surprise of the beautiful mix of flowers and plants they find growing.

The waterfalls took an entire winter to construct. We searched a number of quarries to find a deep yellow stone, and with help from the people from GrowWell (a project for people who have been mental health patients) cut into the bank to make an upper and lower pool, with two streams running between them – streams of life-giving water. By the upper pool is a hut which faces the dawn at Easter time. The floor of the hut is made of recycled plastic, the walls of living willow. It is at the highest point in the garden.

All through the resurrection garden we try to have white or yellow flowers at all seasons, and the beech hedge gives a warm glow throughout the winter.

Each of our gardens has an environmental theme in synergy with the spirituality for that garden. In the resurrection garden the environmental theme is woodland, particularly deciduous woodland, so we have a small tree nursery there where we pot-on tree seedlings that we find. When these are large enough they will be planted locally; some are already planted alongside a local canal. Trees renew the air from pollution, trapping dust so it falls to the ground and releasing oxygen.

Symbols of resurrection are all around us if we have eyes to see, but best are the stories we can tell from our own lives, because resurrection is for now as well as eternity.

Chris Polhill

Deep in the heart of God

Deep in the heart of God there lurks
A mischief making note,
A gurgle of suppressed delight
A chuckle in the throat.
Deep in the heart of God there lies
A reservoir of pain,
A cross-marked agony of love
Filled and refilled again.

God of our laughter and our tears,
Transcending human thought,
You share our fun in life, our fears,
– By incarnation brought:
Father of Jesus Christ, the clown,
Whose Spirit gives us breath,
Hear us, who look to you to crown
Our merriment, our death.

Ian M Fraser

Sources and acknowledgements

Pg 18   'Sing hey for the Carpenter' – from *Love From Below: Wild Goose Songs, Volume 1*, Wild Goose Publications, first published 1989, ISBN 0947988343.

Pg 22   'The desert waits (an invitation to Lent)' – first published in *Bread of Tomorrow: Praying With the World's Poor*, edited by Janet Morley, SPCK, 1992, ISBN 0281045593.

Pg 38   'Transporting goods Sudanese-style' – adapted by Chris Polhill from *Practical Answers to Poverty (Rural Transport)*, a leaflet produced by the Intermediate Technology and Development Group (ITDG). Used by permission of ITDG. (The Intermediate Technology and Development Group works in partnership with communities to develop practical answers to their problems, based on local knowledge and skills and putting people's needs first. The tools used may be simple or sophisticated – but to provide long-term, appropriate and practical answers, they must be firmly in the hands of local people: people who shape technology and control it for themselves. For more information about the Intermediate Technology Development Group (ITDG) visit their website: www.itdg.org or write to the Schumacher Centre for Technology and Development, Bourton Hall, Bourton-on-Dunsmore, Rugby CV23 9QZ, UK. Description of ITDG and information taken from ITDG.)

Pg 44   'Crescent-shaped terraces' – adapted by Chris Polhill from *Practical Answers to Poverty (Food Security in North Darfur)*, a leaflet produced by the Intermediate Technology and Development Group. Used by permission of ITDG.

         'Stemming the flood waters in Bangladesh' – adapted by Chris Polhill from *Small World* magazine, issue 37, Spring 2004, published by the Intermediate Technology and Development Group. Used by permission of ITDG.

Pg 50   'Grid-free power (Wind generation for developing countries)' – Adapted by Chris Polhill from *Hands On Winds of Change – Sri Lanka*. Used by permission of ITDG.

Pg 53   'Objects' – first published in *The Flow: Poetry from Camas*, edited by Rachel McCann, 2003.

Pg 55   'Chip fat fuels lorries' – adapted by Chris Polhill from Information from Global Commodities www.globeco.co.uk

Pg 63   'Look in our hearts, Lord Christ, we pray' – © 1994 Stainer and Bell, words by Ian M Fraser, music by Donald Rennie, from *A Try-it-Out Hymnbook*, Ian M Fraser and Donald Rennie.

Pg 70   'Agricultural biodiversity in India' – Adapted from *Hands On Gene Savers – India*. Used by permission of ITDG.

Pg 82   'Come God and meet us now' – first published in *Cherish the Earth: Reflections on a Living Planet* , Mary Low, Wild Goose Publications, 2003, ISBN 1901557715.

Pg 104   'Searching' – first published in *At Ground Level*, Ruth Burgess, Wild Goose Publications (out of print).

Pg 105   'Credo' by Frances Copsey has previously appeared on the Stanbrook Abbey website.

Pg 106   'A bit of hope, Lent 2004' – first published in the *Coracle* magazine, under the title 'A suburban tale'. The *Coracle* magazine is published by The Iona Community, 4th Floor, Savoy House, 140 Sauchiehall Street, Glasgow G2 3DH coracle@gla.iona.org.uk or www.iona.org.uk/coracle

Pg 112   'Broken' – used by permission of John Coleman and Willow Connection, Australia.

Pg 118   'For the word of God in scripture (responses)' – from *A Wee Worship Book*, Wild Goose Worship Group, Wild Goose Publications, 1999, ISBN 1901557235.

Pg 119   'Gladly we pray' – © 1994 Stainer and Bell, words and melody by Ian M Fraser, music arranged by Donald Rennie, from *A Try-it-Out Hymnbook*, Ian M Fraser and Donald Rennie.

Pg 128   'Oh where are you going' – from *Love From Below: Wild Goose Songs, Volume 1*, Wild Goose Publications, first published 1989, ISBN 0947988343.

Pg 145   'Bird's-eye view' – first published in *Imaginary Conversations: Dialogues for Worship and Bible Study*, Jan Sutch Pickard, Methodist Church Overseas Division, 1989/90.

Pg 186   'Via Dolorosa', 'Women at the wall', 'Church of the Holy Sepulchre', 'The flowers of the field' – from the collection *Holy Places: Gatherings 2*, by Jan Sutch Pickard, Oystercatcher Press, 2004, ISBN 0954555813. Available from Oystercatcher Press, 3 The Village, Bunessan, Isle of Mull PA76 6DG. Profits from the sale of *Holy Places* will be given to projects such as the Palestinian YMCA appeal to plant olive trees: Keep Hope Alive, or to the Growing Hope appeal of the Iona Community. Cost £2.50 (including postage).

Pg 210 'Safe now in God's hands' (Words of remembrance) – first published in *The Book of a Thousand Prayers*, edited by Angela Ashwin, Marshall Pickering, an imprint of Harper Collins, 1996, ISBN 0551028653.

Pg 212 'Dust, dust and ashes' – first published in *Sing Round the Year*, Donald Swann, Bodley Head, 1965, ISBN 370010701. 'This carol was taught to the boys of Sevenoaks School by Joshua Sempebwa who had learned it in Uganda.' (from *Sing Round the Year*)

Pg 214 'Not beyond my ken' – arrangement of tune © James Ross for Coronach. 'Panmure courante' from *Panmure Lute Book (Panmure 5)* c.1632. 'After the paunges of a desperate lover' from *The Balcarres Lute Book* of c.1700.

Pg 230 'This is the Good News' – © Wild Goose Resource Group. From *Stages on the Way*, Wild Goose Publications, 1998, ISBN 1901557111. 'We gather in God's name' and 'Lead us Lord' © Iona Community.

Pg 242 'Deep in the heart of God' – words by Ian M Fraser © 1994 Stainer and Bell, from *A Try-it-Out Hymnbook*, Ian M Fraser and Donald Rennie. Music by Marlene Phillips © 1995 Stainer and Bell, from *Worship Live*, Volume 1, No. 2.

Note: The editors have drawn some material from a creative writing week held on Iona in 1998 but have been unable to trace all the writers. Please contact the publisher if you recognise your work; attributions will be included in future editions.

The Bible readings in *Eggs & Ashes* have been taken from or drawn from the following Bibles: *The New Revised Standard Version*, *The Good News Bible*, *The New English Bible*, *The New International Version*.

Notes

1   Description of the International Development and Technology Group (ITDG) taken from ITDG literature.

2   'What reinforces the Pharisee in you?' – from *Imagining the Gospels*, Kathy Galloway, SPCK, 1988.

3   'Dazzling darkness' – from the poem 'The Night' by Henry Vaughan (1621–95), from *Penguin English Poets Series*, edited by Alan Rudrum, Penguin, 1976.

Index of authors (with page numbers)

About the authors

Stuart Barrie is a retired engineer now serving apprenticeship at 'sitting quietly staring at nothing' and 'visiting the delectable mountains on the wings of laughter'.

Elizabeth Baxter is joint Executive Director of Holy Rood House, Centre for Health and Pastoral Care, in Thirsk, North Yorkshire, and the Centre for the Study of Theology and Health. As a priest and counsellor, she accompanies people on their therapeutic and spiritual journeys. Her liturgy springs from these experiences.

Alix Brown is an independent therapist working with adolescents in the care system. She lives in Shropshire with her partner and a range of animals.

Ruth Burgess is a writer and editor who lives in the North East of England with a large and hungry black and white cat. She is currently working part time with the Alzheimer's Society supporting people with memory loss. She likes fireworks and growing flowers and food. Ruth is a member of the Iona Community.

David Coleman is parent to Taliesin and Melangell, married to Zam, and works with Barrhead United Reformed Church, near Glasgow. He longs to see a fully inclusive, united free catholic Church, and enjoys experimenting in making worship a more audio visually enriching experience, in order to uncover the subversive potential of orthodox Christianity. He is a member of the Iona Community.

John Coleman is an Australian singer/songwriter who has produced a number of CDs in the gospel/folk genre. He is also a long-term member of L'Arche (an International federation of faith communities that have people with an intellectual disability at the heart). John's songs are very much inspired by the lived spirituality of L'Arche and are used in many L'Arche communities around the world. CDs can be purchased by contacting region@larche.org.au – the profits going to support the work of L'Arche in Australia.

Frances Copsey – 'I continue to struggle with words and MS, and now with the Internet too!' More poems by Frances Copsey at www.msplus.pwp.blueyonder.co.uk

Ian Cowie has been a farm labourer, a lieutenant (in the Seaforth Highlanders), and a minister. He is married to Ailsa. They have 5 children and 7 grandchildren and live in Kinross, Scotland. His books include *Jesus' Healing Work and Ours* and *Prayers and Ideas for Healing Services*, both published by Wild Goose.

Andrew De Smet is an Anglican priest, Warden of Offa House, the Coventry Diocesan Retreat House and Conference Centre and a counsellor. He is married with four children and one car, so bicycles come in useful!

Ian M Fraser – 'Margaret married me, I have three children, nine grandchildren and one great-grandchild. I have been a member of the Iona Community since 1941.'

Kathy Galloway is the current Leader of the Iona Community. She is the author/ editor of several books including *Dreaming of Eden, Pushing the Boat Out, Starting Where We Are, The Pattern of Our Days, Praying for the Dawn* (with Ruth Burgess) and *The Dream of Learning Our True Name*, all published by Wild Goose Publications.

Louise Glen-Lee is 33, the same age as our Lord when he died. She is currently working as deputy warden for the Iona Community. She enjoys fashion and twelve bars of chocolate a day.

Bob Green: 'I am a retired pastor of the Christian Church (Disciples of Christ). I am currently travelling full-time with my wife in a motorhome. We are planning to do this for two to three years to try to see the things we have only read about in this huge country of ours (USA). My wife (also a retired Disciples pastor) and I have three sons and six grandchildren.'

Alma Hamilton is an associate member of the Iona Community. For several years she played an active role in the ecumenical scene in Stevenage and in her Catholic parish and now lives with her husband in Somerset; in both places she has been involved in work with the homeless. She has three grown children and six grandchildren of different shapes and sizes.

John Harvey is a member of the Iona Community and lives in Glasgow. A minister in the Church of Scotland, he has worked in Glasgow, Stirling, Iona, Greenock and Edinburgh, and is now officially retired.

Ruth Harvey is a member of the Iona Community and editor of *Coracle* magazine.

Judith Jardine has lived on Iona for over 20 years and finds that every day on the island brings an abundance of privileges and unexpected challenges.

Kirsty Langlands is now aged 20, and is a biochemistry student at Aberdeen University.

Pat Livingstone is a composer and music educator in London. Recent work includes: 'Bathtime Boogie' for prepared piano; 'And the Bread', an Easter play with music for children; 'Winter Lights', for large mixed ensemble; *Brass All Year Round*, a tutor book for young brass players; 'I Saw A Stranger', a CD published by Wild Goose Publications; 'I Want to Be a Millionaire', for the London lesbian and gay chamber choir – Diversity – and reflections in the book *Let Justice Roll Down*, edited by Geoffrey Duncan.

Yvonne Morland is a poet and writer of liturgical and other material. Her writing is largely inspired by the process of trying to live a faith-full life while retaining an open and inclusive heart in this time of many trials in our world. Yvonne is a member of the Iona Community and glad to be part of a laughing, dancing, singing group of people who also seek to live the justice of the Gospel in today's world.

Jean Murdoch died in spring 2003. She lived in Oban and was an associate member of the Iona Community. Her work also appears in *A Book of Blessings* and in *Friends and Enemies*, both published by Wild Goose Publications.

da Noust is an informal circle of members and friends of L'Arche Edinburgh. L'Arche is an ecumenical community welcoming adults with learning difficulties, assistants and others to a shared life. The word Noust is Orcadian for a boat shelter on the shore, a place to withdraw for rest and renewal, prior to setting out fishing once more in the morning. For more information about L'Arche please contact L'Arche Edinburgh, 132 Constitution Street, Edinburgh EH6 6AJ.   da_noust@yahoo.co.uk

Neil Paynter is the editor/author of *Lent & Easter Readings from Iona*, *This is the Day*, and *Blessed Be Our Table*, all published by Wild Goose Publications. In 2003, he was a finalist in the Daily Record's nation wide comedy competition 'Search For A Stand-up Star'. He lives in Biggar, Scotland. For many years he worked in the social care field.

Jan Sutch Pickard is a poet, storyteller and Methodist local preacher, who for five and a half years worked for the Iona Community on Iona, latterly as warden.

Chris Polhill was one of the first women priests in the Church of England, and this year (2004) celebrates 20 years in ministry and 10 years as a priest. She currently works in the Lichfield diocese as a member of a team ministry, and on a Reflections project (five gardens on the Christian spiritual journey) with her husband, John. (Visit the gardens at www.reflectiongardens.org.uk) She is a member of the Iona Community and a frequent contributor to Wild Goose books.

Gary Polhill is a scientist and lives in Aberdeen.

John Polhill is a member of the Iona Community.

Jo Rathbone is married with two children. She says, 'As a family we try to make choices that are good for the planet and its people, particularly walking, cycling and using public transport.'

Donald Rennie is a member of the Iona Community.

Josie Smith has been a teacher, a freelance radio and TV broadcaster, a Methodist preacher, and worked for 13 years on the staff of the Methodist headquarters. She is now actively retired in Sheffield.

Andrew Softley completed university in 2003 and is currently working as a town planner. He says of writing his contribution to this book: 'My memories of the day were of enjoyment and also accomplishment as we worked together as a community to give the Easter story a modern twist … I'm grateful I was able to partake in it.'

Liz Varley is a parish priest in North Yorkshire and an associate member of the Iona Community.

Emily Walker is a musician living in London. She worked for the Iona Community in 2003–04, as the musician of Iona Abbey.

Brian Woodcock is a United Reformed Church minister in St Albans. He is a member of the Iona Community and was warden of Iona Abbey from 1998 to 2001.

The Iona Community

The Iona Community, founded in 1938 by the Revd George MacLeod, then a parish minister in Glasgow, is an ecumenical Christian community committed to seeking new ways of living the Gospel in today's world. Initially working to restore part of the medieval abbey on Iona, the Community today remains committed to 'rebuilding the common life' through working for social and political change, striving for the renewal of the church with an ecumenical emphasis, and exploring new, more inclusive approaches to worship, all based on an integrated understanding of spirituality.

The Community now has over 240 Members, about 1500 Associate Members and around 1500 Friends. The Members – women and men from many denominations and backgrounds (lay and ordained), living throughout Britain with a few overseas – are committed to a fivefold Rule of devotional discipline, sharing and accounting for use of time and money, regular meeting, and action for justice and peace.

At the Community's three residential centres – the Abbey and the MacLeod Centre on Iona, and Camas Adventure Camp on the Ross of Mull – guests are welcomed from March to October and over Christmas. Hospitality is provided for over 110 people, along with a unique opportunity, usually through week-long programmes, to extend horizons and forge relationships through sharing an experience of the common life in worship, work, discussion and relaxation. The Community's shop on Iona, just outside the Abbey grounds, carries an attractive range of books and craft goods.

The Community's administrative headquarters are in Glasgow, which also serves as a base for its work with young people, the Wild Goose Resource Group working in the field of worship, a bi-monthly magazine, *Coracle*, and a publishing house, Wild Goose Publications.

For information on the Iona Community contact:
The Iona Community, Fourth Floor, Savoy House, 140 Sauchiehall Street, Glasgow G2 3DH,
UK. Phone: 0141 332 6343
e-mail: ionacomm@gla.iona.org.uk; web: www.iona.org.uk

For enquiries about visiting Iona, please contact:
Iona Abbey, Isle of Iona, Argyll PA76 6SN, UK. Phone: 01681 700404
e-mail: ionacomm@iona.org.uk

Wild Goose Publications, the publishing house of the Iona Community established in the Celtic Christian tradition of Saint Columba, produces books, tapes and CDs on:

- holistic spirituality
- social justice
- political and peace issues
- healing
- innovative approaches to worship
- song in worship, including the work of the Wild Goose Resource Group
- material for meditation and reflection

If you would like to find out more about our books, tapes and CDs, please contact us at:

Wild Goose Publications
Fourth Floor, Savoy House
140 Sauchiehall Street,
Glasgow G2 3DH, UK

Tel. +44 (0)141 332 6292
Fax +44 (0)141 332 1090
e-mail: admin@ionabooks.com

or visit our website at
www.ionabooks.com
for details of all our products and online sales